Transforming Power

Stories from Transformational Leaders for
Encouragement and Inspiration

Compiled and Edited
by

Hugh Ballou

D1609269

DISCIPLESHIP RESOURCES

P O BOX 340003 • NASHVILLE, TN 37203-0003
www.discipleshipresources.org

Library of Congress Cataloging-in-Publication Data

Transforming power : stories from transformational leaders for encouragement and inspiration / compiled and edited by Hugh Ballou.
    p. cm.
  ISBN 978-0-88177-531-0
  1. Leadership--Religious aspects--Christianity. 2. Organizational change. I. Ballou, Hugh, 1946-
   BV4597.53.L43T725 2008
   253--dc22

                              2008013902

ISBN 978-0-88177-531-0

TABLE OF CONTENTS

The Transformational Leader

The process of collecting these essays was a transformational experience for me. I gave the same information to each person. Each of us experiences transformation as we see it and can only report it from our own perspective. Therefore this collection contains a wide variety of perspectives representing many types of transformation. The contributors all responded with their own unique perspectives and through their own personal styles of writing and from their individual leadership perspectives.

What is consistent among these essays is that each story will inspire or encourage some leader attempting to transform an organization, and to make a difference in the lives of people under his or her leadership. We are challenged as leaders to help those whom we lead to grow in their own leadership ability, but we must change ourselves first. If we expect transformation from others, we must be willing to transform ourselves.

Transformational Leadership was birthed from the writings of B. M. Bass and J. M. Burns. Burns sees transformational leadership linked with high order values while Bass does not see it with any moral connection at all. Bass and Burns are extensively quoted and their writings are a referral source for papers and theories on this style of leadership. In practicality, there is a unique set of qualities for this profile. The transformational leader:

Shares responsibilities

Promotes creativity

Defines goals

Delegates effectively

Coaches others

Celebrates accomplishments

Provides knowledge

Values individuals

Models leadership

Articles on leadership compare transformational leadership, transactional leadership, charismatic leadership, servant leadership and other styles that leaders follow. The fine points of each, the weaknesses of each, as well as the benefits of each are the subject of much debate. The traits for the transformational leader listed above will serve as the model for this book, and it is the model I sent each writer to ponder as they considered writing a story for inclusion herein.

As you will see, not every leader possesses each of these traits. Are they still a transformational leader? In my view, they are if there is some transformation present, even if that transformation is in their own life, leadership style, or personality.

In the best sense, transformational leaders equip and create community. This community generates synergy by building on the trust and consensus created through the integrity of leadership. This integrity is not only a moral high point in ethical behavior, but integrity in the relationship—a collaborative relationship. The standard is created as the leader models this for the community. The vision is articulated and clarified as momentum is created, moving the community toward the common goals set by the team and modified by that team. The transformational leader controls the process by power of integrity, not power of position. Veto power is maintained by the transformational leader, but is rarely needed. Effective communication, planning, and delegation results in fewer, if any, uses of that veto by the leader.

Transformational leaders are not intimidated by teams, committees, or boards, but *lead* those groups to fulfilling the vision through mutual accountability, open and honest communication, and effective planning. Empowering groups to take charge in specific areas is a model for strong leadership, not weakness as some might fear. Every leader has gaps in his or her own skill set. Being honest with the team about those gaps requires that the leader posses strong self-esteem and confidence about the skill set he or she *does* have. In fact, team members know quite well what those gaps are and some will be able to add complementing strengths. As a conductor must be willing to be vulnerable on the podium in order to make great music, the leader must be vulnerable to release full cooperation of the team.

The transforming leadership model requires that the leader think thoroughly through process. Process builds trust. Process creates community. Process itself is a unifying collaborative force. The leader, like a conductor of a great orchestra, knows where the final cadence lies. The pace (tempo) is clearly articulated, with a detailed action plan (the music). The conductor continues to be fully in charge without taking over the oboe solo, or crashing the symbols, or interfering with the consummate skill of those recruited to complete the symphony. The conductor allows them to create magnificence within this detailed structure. The musical leadership parallel of this is that the players (team members) are part of creating the music itself and then they will play that music together as they become the "ensemble" (a "community").

Since music is a creative process within an extremely exacting framework, it is not a fully compatible example; however, the fundamental concept is quite similar. Get good people and let them do what you've asked them to do! Get out of their way! Set clear objectives, accountabilities, and timelines. Delegation is not an absence of leadership skill or authority. The Transformational Leader is a leader in control and fully present in the expansion of creative energy.

Working on a church staff for 40 years has given me a unique perspective on leadership. Clergy are trained in theology, but are expected to be experts in leadership by virtue of their position. The role they are forced into as leader, pastor, motivator, administrator, and head of staff is not comfortable for everyone or practical for anyone. Therefore the effective pastor, as well as the successful business and community leader, becomes more effective as they learn to empower those whom they lead.

The stories that follow demonstrate transformations in different venues and in many different forms. From ministering to children to being in prison to making Hollywood movies, leaders *lead*.

These stories are here to inspire and encourage leaders who want to transform organizations and make a difference. Just as the conductor steps in front of the orchestra for a rehearsal knowing clearly what sounds are to be created, the leader also creates something out of nothing beginning with a vision, an idea, or a concept. The *way* to the end is not always clear. However, the final *result* must be clear. The conductor will use numerous techniques to allow the players to grasp the vision, the exact genius that makes music so special. The leader must also be willing to allow course corrections, especially those offered by the team itself.

Imbedded in every story is a personal statement of faith. God planted a vision with each leader. God has inspired each leader with a unique vision. Each leader in this book stepped up to a call to action.

Create and maintain the high standard. Then, let the team go there.

PAUL BORDEN

Paul Borden is the Executive Minister of Growing Healthy Churches, formerly American Baptist Churches of the West. This region of 220 congregations saw over 70% of their churches transformed and is now focusing on congregational reproduction through out the United States and around the world. The region is planting ten churches a year, many starting with 200-500 people at launch. Paul has authored two successfully selling books *Hit the Bullseye* and *Direct Hit*. Both books are written to explain how denominations, congregations, and pastors can once again be effective and see health and growth. Paul has been asked to train, consult, or speak to over 40 different denominational groups in the United States, Canada, Australia, and New Zealand. He is currently implementing with denominations an effective strategy that is helping them see significant transformation in what were dying congregations.

New Wine Is Needed to Burst Old Wineskins

(The following story is true. Names and details have been changed to protect the guilty)

Edward and Taylor with their young family, were invited to old First Church to lead change. Old First Church had seen its glory days over a decade before they arrived. Back then, the congregation averaged over 500 in worship and many in the community attended for both spiritual and social reasons. The people were proud of their building and the influence the church had in the community. However, the numbers had dwindled and by the time Edward and his family arrived the congregation averaged around 70 in worship. The younger families had left and there were no children under five in the church, with only two or three teens who attended any events offered for the youth. Sunday morning worship was lifeless and the Christian Education facility was locked.

Prior to Edward's arrival, the denominational official had led the congregation through a congregational assessment and told the people it was time to either change or die. The current pastor was provided a chance to lead change, but he simply did not possess the gifts and talents for such a task. After six months, the congregation's leaders met with the denominational official and informed him that the kind of change envisioned would not occur with the current pastor. As a result, the denominational official helped the pastor resign well and leave in a way that honored both him and the congregation.

The denominational official then began to look for a pastor who was a leader, who was leading a healthy, growing congregation, and who would be open to coming to First Church and take on a major challenge. Edward and his family were introduced to the lay leaders and the congregation, and they invited him to become their pastor and lead change. Edward accepted the challenge.

Within a year and a half of Edward's coming, major changes had occurred. The congregation had grown from 70 to 200. Many of the brand new attendees were clueless about church life since the reason they were coming was that they had recently become first-time disciples of Jesus Christ. The atmosphere was electric, worship was exciting, and the congregation once again had momentum.

It was at this point that severe problems began to emerge. The older people in the church who had wanted change, felt the congregation needed a new pastor, and wanted to see their church alive again were very dissatisfied with all that was happening. First, the new people were not like them or like their friends, who over the last ten years had left the church. The worship style was changing and the congregation no longer felt like their church. The new people did not share their social and cultural values, and these long-time members realized they were losing control.

These people went to their pastor and asked him to stop all that he was doing, even though they had asked him to come to lead change and help create new life and growth. When he refused, their anger over the situation shifted from what was happening in the congregation to their pastor. This started a campaign to get the pastor to leave.

Each week key members would go to the pastor's office and ask him to resign. They went to one of their denomination's national leaders and asked him to get the pastor to resign. He also refused their request. They then appealed to their national denominational leaders, telling them their pastor had been brought in under false pretenses, had a criminal record, and that the local denominational officials were doing nothing about these grievous behaviors.

Those who were disgruntled began email, phone, and letter campaigns asking the rest of the congregation, including many of the new people to join them in their efforts to oust the pastor and his family. They even developed a weekly newsletter describing how bad their congregation was and how poorly their pastor was treating the congregation. They then distributed the newsletters each Sunday to those entering the church for worship, including visitors.

The pastor finally met with two local denominational officials and told them of an upcoming congregational meeting for which the pastor had hired off-duty policemen to attend, fearing for his safety and that of others who would be in attendance. These two officials supported the pastor and helped him map out a strategy, not only for the meeting, but also how to deal with the ten ring leaders (who had thirty others aligned with them) leading all this discontent.

The pastor followed the strategies, and as a result led other long-time members, who sided with the pastor and embraced the growth, to oust the malcontents from the congregation. When the ten were asked to leave, the other thirty people, who sided with them, left as well. However, all of these actions came with great pain and created a toxic situation for the congregation. By the time the dust had settled, the congregation had gone back to about 130 in worship, the budget was in shambles, since many who left took their offerings with them, and the pastor and his family were deeply and severely bruised both spiritually and emotionally.

Those who left did not go quietly into the dark night. They continued to communicate with national denominational leaders telling them about how poorly they had been treated. They also attempted to create problems with nearby congregations. And they attended denominational meetings bearing signs communicating that they had been banished from their congregation.

However, God was not done with this pastor and the people who were left. After all the disgruntled members left, the congregation began again to grow. Within another year and a half the congregation was pushing 300 in worship. It was at this time God performed a miracle and provided some unplanned and unexpected publicity for the congregation in the community. This publicity caused the congregation to almost double overnight. Today this congregation, in four services on the weekend, ministers to over 1,000 people. Many of the new people who attend were not disciples of Jesus Christ three or four years ago. However, they have found a congregation that not only welcomes them but seeks to remove as many as possible of the cultural boundaries people often have to cross to meet Jesus Christ. Probably 95% of those attending the church when the changes started are no longer there.

This story has been repeated over 100 times in congregations within our local region of our denominational churches. This story is the most extreme in terms of the behaviors described. However the pain in leading similar changes in our congregations has been experienced by all those pastors and their families who have followed this pattern.

Lessons We Have Learned in Leading Transformation

1. Congregations that have been on a plateau or in decline for more than three years are like old drunks. Intervention is needed to produce change. Without intervention these congregations will continue to be disobedient to God's Great Commission for the Church.

2. Leadership is essential. The pastor must be a leader or have the ability to exercise leadership behavior. However, most pastors cannot lead such change alone. Pastors need help from the outside. A key and fundamental role for denominational personnel is to stand with leader pastors and risk the loss of congregational dollars and affirmation.

3. Pastors and denominations that do not want to disrupt comfortable congregations must understand they are abdicating their responsibilities as Christian leaders to serve God well. Enabling and helping congregations to continually exercise sinful dysfunctional behavior means that such pastors and denominational leaders are practicing carnal co-dependent relationships that work against God's mission for the Church.

4. The ultimate issues in congregations that fight and resist change relates ultimately to people wanting to hold and control the power (to influence the congregation), money, and turf.

5. Leading congregational transformation is much more difficult than starting new congregations. However, the investment is worth it when one sees expensive facilities sitting on valuable properties being used to achieve grand missions that produce changed lives and communities.

6. There are only two valid reasons for denominations to exist. One is to help congregations transform and the second is to then help them reproduce. Denominations play other key managerial and administrative roles. But if the mission is not prominent in terms of how resources are expended in our nation and in nations around the world, then denominations have no right to exist.

7. Most pastors are unwilling as well as incapable of leading the kind of systemic change that is demonstrated in this story. This is why they need help to both know what to do and to have someone stand with them as they do it. The bottom line is all about leadership and pastors being willing to be or act like leaders who risk their jobs if necessary.

8. The cost is terrible until one achieves the change. After the change comes, the pastor finally gets to lead ministry in ways that all pastors imagined they would when they entered seminary. However, the biggest cost to leading change is usually borne by the pastor and the pastor's family. In many cases the attacks are personal and are unrelated to the issues that are being addressed with the congregation. Married couples soon find out the venom that comes is splashed over the entire family (including children), rather than just being directed like a laser towards the pastor.

9. There is a major difference between creating changes that lead to systemic change and leading systemic change. However, the more presystemic change that is implemented the easier it will be to lead systemic change. Pastors, particularly those who do not have outside help may need to make small, incremental changes for one to five years before leading systemic change. However, once systemic change is initiated, the pastor has only from one to two years to make it happen. It may then take another three to five years to make sure the congregation does not go back to old ways of behaving.

10. Congregations who say they want change mean something different from what most pastors think. What congregations mean by wanting change is that they want more people in church and more money in the budget as long as the culture of the congregation does not change and they can still be in control of how things are done. The biggest cost to any change is getting the congregation out of the hands of those who have been running the congregation for years. However, when such happens we have seen awesome results.

Congregational transformation comes when such systematic changes occur that the very culture of the old is replaced by the new. The new culture is like new wine. And that new wine does not enter into the old culture gently and without stress. In most cases, the stress is so severe that the old wineskin must burst. The few pastors who are leaders can do this on their own. However, all pastors who want to lead can see this change occur if their denominational leaders will stand with them. That means that pastors, lay leaders, and denominational leaders must be willing to go through the stress of bursting old wineskins in order to see the new wine bubble forth with life and vitality.

LARRY DILL

L arry Dill has been Executive Director of the Institute for Clergy Excellence since February 1, 2003. He and his wife, Peggy, are the parents of two sons, Randy and David, and grandparents of Ella.

Larry was born in Tuscaloosa, Alabama and grew up in a Methodist pastor's family. He is a graduate of Birmingham-Southern College where he majored in History/Political Science. He completed his seminary training at Candler School of Theology, Emory University, Atlanta, where he received the M.Div. with a major in Systematic Theology and the D.Min. in worship and preaching. He served as pastor of rural, sububan, new church, and urban appointments prior to appointment in 1994 to Trinity United Methodist Church, Huntsville, Alabama.

Larry is a member of Leadership Birmingham and Leadership Huntsville/Madison County. He is a past president of the Minister's Association of Greater Birmingham and of Eastside Mental Health Center. In 1987, he was chosen Citizen of the Year by the Eastern Area Chamber of Commerce in Birmingham, Alabama.

Cappuccino and Christ

We were sitting in the conference room. The shadows of a late fall day lengthened. A half dozen experts on marketing and public relations had hurried to an after work meeting. As their pastor, I had called on them to plan the publicity for a new worship service. Most were unaccustomed to meeting like this. They were not your usual church committee members. But, they felt honored to be called by their church to lend professional expertise to a new project.

I explained that we planned to initiate a new worship service. It would be held in the church fellowship hall, encourage casual dress, be filled with contemporary Christian music, and be aimed toward attracting new people. I asked these professionals to lay out a strategy of public advertisement that would attract a large crowd on the first Sunday of the new venture.

They immediately seized on the matter of the new people. "Who are you trying to reach?" they asked. I gave the rather thin answer, "Folks who are not presently attending worship." But it was enough. Like a pack of dogs thrown a bone, they grabbed at this idea with an increasingly animated conversation. Finally someone said, "Would it be the person who is sitting home on Sunday morning, drinking cappuccino and reading the paper?" "Yes," I said, "that's it."

Presently, after some technical talk, such as, "Well then, any newspaper ads should be in the Sunday paper," the group began talking about what to call the service. And then came the momentous insight, "Why don't we call it Cappuccino and Christ?" Looking at me they asked, "Can we do that?" "Sure, why not?" I replied.

The phrase "Cappuccino and Christ" was intended to be an advertising soundbite. A marketing hook intended to evangelize a new population, however, became the name of a new congregation imbedded in a 40-year-old suburban church. Within a few months Cappuccino and Christ doubled the weekly worship attendance and boosted the church to the top attendance in the Conference. Had it been a freestanding new church, it would have been in the top five weekly attendance congregations.

Church staff and laity invented a new strategy for evangelism that worked to draw a new constituency. This church within a church, which very soon became affectionately known as C&C, was different.

It dearly loved the Eucharist and Baptism.

Worshippers did not seen to know to stay away on holidays.

C&C participants could not help but invite family, co-workers, neighbors, and friends to attend with them.

Teenagers and elementary school kids brought their parents and grandparents.

They laughed, they cried, they clapped, they made worship fun.

This Is The Story of a Leadership Partnership

In 1994 I became pastor of a large-membership congregation in a medium-sized city. The church was about to celebrate its 40th Anniversary. I brought with me the idea of a new worship format that would include different music, less traditional liturgy, and a more casual feel. Within a few months the staff and selected lay leaders began discussing the possibilities for such a new worship experience.

Church consultant Herb Miller had been booked by my predecessor for a regional ecumenical workshop to be held at the church. Our staff negotiated an additional half day with him to discuss several issues including our plan for the new worship experiment. Miller encouraged us to move forward and said, in his characteristically direct way, "There are two Sundays of the year to begin a new worship service—the Sunday after Labor Day or the first Sunday in Lent." We took this to be good advice, worked 18 months to get ready, and on the First Sunday in Lent 1996, Cappuccino and Christ met for the first time with 500 people in attendance.

For six weeks prior to this first gathering, I made the same announcement. It went something like this:

The first Sunday in Lent we are beginning a new worship service in the church fellowship hall. Its purpose is to attract new people to Jesus Christ and this congregation. The time of the service will be the same time as our Sunday School because that seems to be the most ideal time to draw the people we are hoping to reach. So, I have a special request of you. During Lent, for the sake of evangelism (winning people to Jesus Christ), I'm asking you to give up one week of Sunday School and attend the new service. I am asking this for two reasons. First, we want to draw a large crowd of people to the service so that the new people we are able to attract will be excited, energized, and impressed. Your attendance will give us the critical mass we need to get the worship experience off to a strong start. Second, I want you to know what we are doing down in the basement. It will be the same sermon, same Scripture, same theological approach that we take in the sanctuary. The dress, music, and format will be different, but I want you to see that the gospel will be the same.

As the weeks passed I thought to add two images.

In 1 Corinthians 9:22-23 we read: "I have become all things to all people, that I might by all means save some. I do it all for the sake of the gospel, so that I may share in its blessings." It is not easy to reach people for Jesus Christ. Paul said, ". . . that I might by all means save some . . ." By adding variety to the way we worship and communicate we are following the Bible's instruction to "become all things to all people."

Those of us who have more than one child know that it is possible to bring new children into the family and love them without taking away any love from the children we already have. Parents expecting their second child often wonder how this can be. I remember thinking it just cannot be true that I will love my second child as much as I love my first born. Of course, I found out quickly what parents for generations have known. I think it is a little like that as we anticipate starting a new worship service. In a true sense, it is like welcoming a new child into the family. We already have two children: the 8:30 service and the 10:50 service. Cappuccino and Christ is a new baby being born into our family. We can love that new baby without taking away any love from our older children.

On the first Sunday in Lent 1996, 500 people packed into the church fellowship hall for C&C. Veteran crowd counters estimated that approximately 300 were church members, many who had given up their Sunday School class for Lent. But there were also approximately 200 new people! And the 200 we had never seen before, had no idea that the 300 were "plants." C&C was off to a roaring start. We all woke up in a new world on the Monday after the first Sunday in Lent.

For at least eight weeks we made no "churchy" sounding announcements. During the greeting and announcement time we said, "We are glad you are here today, we hope you will come back next Sunday and invite someone to come with you." For more than 20 years I had believed the findings of the church growth movement that new people attend a church for the first time—primarily—because they are invited by a neighbor, coworker, or family member. In the congregations I served as pastor I kept that emphasis focused for the people. Always I was inviting church folk to invite, invite, invite. Therefore, it was natural to begin C&C this way. "We are glad you are here, please come back and bring someone with you."

It was not long, however, until I realized I did not need to badger this congregation about this inviting. They were doing it naturally. Because they were so excited, they could not help but invite the people they knew. Around town, people I did not recognize began to speak to me.

A waitress brings back my check with the credit card receipt and says, "I enjoyed your sermon at Cappuccino and Christ last Sunday." "How long have you been attending?" I ask. "About six weeks," she says, "I haven't missed a time since I started." "Why did you come the first time?" I continue. "My friends brought me," she replies.

In the ICU waiting room, off intensive care at the hospital, I'm sitting with a family receiving bad news from a physician. They are crying, already adjusting, and coping the best they can in the tragic moment. A nurse is with us to answer more questions. She and I step out in the hall to let the family have privacy, and she says to me, "That joke you told on Sunday near the end of your sermon, I've told that to several people." I ask my questions: How long? Why did you first attend? She says a co-worker at the hospital invited her.

Standing in the teller's line to cash a check, I get one of the best stories. A young man behind me says, "You don't recognize me, but I come to C&C every Sunday." He said he had been attending over a year and that he first came with his girl friend. He went on to offer that they had broken up but he had continued coming almost every week and had brought at least a dozen friends, mostly from work.

We waited until World Communion Sunday to attempt the Eucharist. I did not know exactly how to approach it so I kept putting it off until something had to be done. By that time C&C had moved from the fellowship hall into the church gym. The worship planning team carefully worked out the logistics. Beautiful loaves, goblets in interesting designs, serving stations around the room, just the right music, intinction, a lean liturgy thrown on the big screen, were the building blocks lovingly put in place. I honestly did not know what to expect. When the invitation to the stations was offered, the people rushed forward. It felt almost like a mob scene. Tears streaming, smiles, hugs, joy in receiving the body and blood of the Lord. The Lord's Supper became the favorite service of C&C. Over the years, I had been tempted to keep the news of an upcoming communion service from my congregation. I sadly realized that if many learned we were having communion they would stay away. But not here! It was just the opposite. If they learned we were offering communion they would come in larger numbers.

We also had the same kind of pleasant surprise when it came to holiday Sundays. I remember approaching the first Labor Day weekend. At breakfast that Sunday morning, my wife and I predicted the C&C crowd would be slim. "They don't have much institutional loyalty," I reasoned. But it didn't happen. The crowd was its normal size. The new reality was tested for sure when the Sunday after Christmas rolled around. Again, a full house despite the holiday! I began to think: Every Methodist knows you don't attend church on holidays, July 4th, Labor Day, three-day holiday weekends, and *especially* the Sunday after Christmas. Everybody knows you don't come to church on holidays! I enjoyed saying, "Don't let the C&C crowd know that Methodists stay home on holidays."

My phone rang one morning and I answered to face a complaint from the father of a teenaged boy. He explained that he wanted his son in youth Sunday School class but the boy refused to go to his class, insisting on attending C&C. The father, who had worked up a head of steam about this, said we should not schedule C&C at the same time as Sunday School. Nothing I could say about our reasons for doing it this way gave him any satisfaction. Finally, exasperated, I said, "Now let me get this straight. You are complaining because your 15-year-old son is begging you every Sunday morning to let him attend worship?"

For the first time in the conversation, he paused. Then more timidly replied, "That's crazy, isn't it?" I said, "Yeah! That's *real* crazy, given the kind of world we live in, which is increasingly dangerous for teenagers. If your kid is pleading with you to let him go to C&C, for goodness sake don't discourage him." Other parents reacted more positively. Several families told stories of teenagers and younger children who were asking during the week if they could go to C&C, getting up early on Sunday morning to get ready to go without the normal hassle, and even inviting parents who were not church goers to attend C&C with them.

Eugene Peterson in *The Message* renders 1 Corinthians 9:19-23 like this:

Even though I am free of the demands and expectations of everyone, I have voluntarily become a servant to any and all in order to reach a wide range of people: religious, nonreligious, meticulous moralists, loose-living immoralists, the defeated, the demoralized—whoever. I didn't take on their way of life. I kept my bearings in Christ—but I entered their world and tried to experience things from their point of view. I've become just about every sort of servant there is in my attempts to lead those I meet into a God-saved life. I did all this because of the Message. I didn't just want to talk about it; I wanted to be in on it.

A partnership of leaders brought this ancient strategy to life in a 21st-century congregation. This story only begins to tell how hundreds of people experienced the gospel in a new way in Cappuccino and Christ, a new church within a 40-year-old congregation. It was said of C&C, "They laughed, they cried, they clapped, they made worship fun." Thanks be to God!

JASON BYASSEE

J ason Byassee holds a Ph.D. in theology from Duke University. He is assistant editor at *Christian Century* magazine, where he writes on such topics as theology, church history, politics, popular culture, and spiritual practices. He has taught at Garrett-Evangelical Theological Seminary, North Park Theological Seminary, Wheaton College, and Northern Seminary. He is author of *Reading Augustine: A Guide to Confessions* (Cascade, 2006), *Praise Seeking Understanding* (Eerdmans, forthcoming) and of an introduction to the *Sayings of the Desert Fathers* (Cascade, forthcoming). He is a probationary elder in the Western North Carolina Conference of the United Methodist Church.

Transformational Leadership in a Prayer Meetin'

The shelves of Barnes & Noble suggest that stories of transformational leadership are about charismatic individuals who heroically bend an organization to their wills, save it from ruin, and deliver it to unending prosperity. As a pastor of a rural church in North Carolina, I found transformational leadership stemming not from me, but from the molasses-sweet, blue-haired, bible-believing old ladies who attended our Wednesday night prayer meeting.

I became pastor of Shady Grove United Methodist Church in Caswell County, North Carolina, just as the politicking was picking up in advance of the 2002 election. This would normally have minimal effect on a congregation's life. In our case the effect was maximal: two members were running against each other for a seat on the county board. The key campaign issue between them was whether to zone Shady Grove Road in an effort to increase property value and attract new development. Charges flew between the two camps: the pro-zoning crowd was considered elitist, the anti-zoning group backward. To make matters worse, the church member/candidate who was pro-zoning came from the church's old money family. The anti-zoning candidate came from the coarser stock of new money. "You got to understand," one observer told me, "the Smiths were all landowners. The Joneses were all sharecroppers." Memories can outrun their usefulness. The Smiths were no longer wealthy; the Joneses no longer poor. But words like "elitist" and "upstart" and "snob" and "white trash" have a way of lingering.

The dispute hurt our church terribly. Longtime members threatened to leave, or at least resign leadership posts (which they left effectively vacant anyway). People worried openly about a church split. In one Administrative Board meeting I found myself with one candidate and his spouse, and the campaign manager of the other and his spouse. The two men had once been dear friends. Their sons still were. They'd known each other since their baptisms. Their parents still talked about how lovely the other's grandparents were. And their dispute wasn't nearly as nasty or personal as that between their wives. The two couples were not even speaking (thankfully, perhaps). Yet we were to pass a budget together? The most painful part was that they were all lovely people, salt-of-the-earth types who still knew how to get their hands dirty and fix a motor, prepare a casserole and teach a Sunday School lesson, but could not, for the life of them (or their pastor), get along.

Amidst the tumult I had to deal with "prayer meetin'," as we North Carolinians call it. When I first became pastor and heard such a meeting existed, I was primed to kill it. I'd insist on having communion each time it met, or be otherwise engaged every Wednesday night, or something, *anything*, to avoid a Baptist-style "sweet hour of prayer." And Baptist it was—every member had been a Baptist at some point (this is common among Methodists in the rural South). Some left when a Baptist church exploded, or over a dispute with a pastor, or whatever. They were (mostly) glad for Methodist polity in which a Bishop can step into a church fight and impose order, as they had all seen Baptist churches dash themselves against the rocks. Though occasionally they were none too happy with where they heard their tithes were going. When the United Methodists made sympathetic noises about gay people or pacifists, they fumed. "Why don't we go independent?" one asked me. "I heard the church is funneling money to the war protestors," another protested.

They longed for that ole' time religion. One would often tell me of a traveling evangelist troupe of some sort that had come through the county decades before. "They had people down the aisles at the altar call, crying, repenting. My husband and I got saved that night." Then she would look at me with a mischievous gleam, "We could have that here you know, if we prayed hard enough." If someone was sick, they'd anoint 'em. If someone not present was sick, they'd anoint someone present as a proxy on the ill person's behalf. One night someone at the prayer meetin' proudly displayed a rock she'd been given at a conference. It had a Star of David on it. "The speaker gave it to us as a reminder that anyone who blesses Israel will be blessed, and if America doesn't bless Israel, we'll be cursed." Another asked me once whether, when the rapture comes, it'll be China that invades the United States, since she heard they had the biggest army in the world. One Sunday a visitor stood up during service and began shouting, "The Lord is going to burn this world up with fire! We better be ready! We needed the gifts of the Holy Ghost!" We waited for him to stop and leave. One of my prayer ladies on her way out of church said to me, "Did you hear him? He says he told us what the Holy Ghost told him to. And I believe him!"

Can you see why a kid from a university town with a freshly-minted Ph.D. didn't want to go to "prayer meetin'"?

But I went, because we sure needed prayer. I could hardly have a conversation with anyone in the community, church member or not, in which the election didn't come up. "Can you believe what Jones said?" "Have you heard what Smith did?" "How can a Christian act that way?" "Do you know his uncle has money and wants this zoning to make more of it?" "You know his brother ran so-and-so's campaign, isn't that awful?" "They had a meeting the other night and they was cussin' and drinkin'—can you believe it?" "They expect me to go to church with those people?" And so on.

In fact, the only people who didn't talk about the election incessantly were the prayer ladies. That's because they were talking about Jesus incessantly, and getting people saved, and healing sick people, and making America more Christian (I'm for all of these, even the last, though it meant something different to me!). When politics came up in prayer meeting, no one was shocked. These women had been through a lot of life, not all of it pretty. They had buried family members and spouses and friends, seen prodigal sons and daughters wander off and never return. That's precisely why they prayed so hard. So they weren't surprised or aghast at what people are capable of doing. They'd seen it all before. They just "lifted it up to the Lord," as they liked to say, letting it weigh on Jesus' shoulders instead of their own.

This isn't to say the prayer ladies didn't have opinions on the election. I could've told you who supported who, who felt like who was being unchristian, whose husband fished with whose daddy and so had their vote. But here's the key: this wasn't the most important thing about them. It wasn't even on the list of the top ten most important things about them. It was just another item on the prayer list: that the church wouldn't be hurt, that souls wouldn't be twisted by the political finagling, that pride at denouncing someone else wouldn't turn into that worst of all sins—pride. They'd seen it happen with the Baptists. They didn't think it could with the Methodists. But an even more important glue for holding the church together than a Bishop was prayer meetin'.

Their example encouraged me. More than that, they got after me. If I hinted that Scripture wasn't as historically reliable as they liked, they let me know about it. If I started doubting that God could do miracles, they set me straight. There was a toughness there that made you quiver if you ran afoul of it. One, who sang in the choir, noticed the choir member behind her wasn't joining in to sing "Praise God" at the right moment. So during the choir's Sunday performance, decked out in blue robes and leading us all in song, she turned around at the right instant and barked at her colleague, "Praise God," with a scowl on her face that signaled she meant it. "It is right to praise God. Now shape up!" Once I tried to defer pastoral authority on some decision or other in the passive-aggressive hope that someone else would make the hard decision. I joked "Don't ask me, I only work here." One came right back: "No you don't, you *lead* here."

Heartened by their example and given ballast by their support, I started praying for our elected leaders in Sunday service, as Christians have always done (even when those leaders were feeding them to lions). I prayed over the election and asked that we would witness to our faith in public in this and in all our lives. Lo and behold, the eighth chapter of Romans came up in the lectionary, with its description of God's "election" of us in Christ, so my sermon title was "The Election." I opened, "No, not that one." And preached that there is another election far more important than this one, which only seemed important. Encouraged by the prayer ladies, our "biggest crisis" was set in perspective. October would come and go, and the church would be here another 100 years to bury these candidates' grandchildren, as long as someone was praying on Wednesday night.

Those women were Shady Grove's transformational leaders. People didn't come to church for the preaching or the programming or the music. They came because of those women. When one told you she was praying for you, it meant something. When one hugged you, you remembered all week. When one cooked for you, the casserole tasted like love. And when you were around them you were in the presence of Jesus. Their presence, their dogged refusal to let the church be merely political, kept the church's fabric from pulling apart at the seams. We were about Jesus, after all, not anything so parochial as a county board election (can someone tell this to the presidential candidates, please?). And the way to stay about Jesus was to forgive like Jesus forgives, to treat enemies like God does—with kindness.

The election didn't turn out well for Smith, the incumbent. He was viewed as too tied in to moneyed interests in the county who stood to gain by the road's rezoning, and was voted out handily. Jones had some missteps early in his commissionership, which Smith reveled in. Smith even ran again two years later for an open, county-wide seat, and lost again. In short the election didn't go away. When we argued about whether and how to build a new parsonage, the argument fell along "party lines." All of Smith's people were for it; Jones' were against it. What did the parsonage have to do with the election? Nothing at all. The grooves in the road were well-worn by then, we just kept barreling along with them.

Except eventually the election did fade from our consciousness. Not because its effects vanished, as I say. But because the church remembered its first job was to be the church, not a political entity. That both Smith and Jones and all their friends and kin belonged there and none would be kicked out for doing something they shouldn't. That the prayer ladies were right: when things are bad, pray. Then pray again. Pray harder. Then pray some more. And "praise God!" already. Do that, and the church will redirect itself toward Jesus and away from its own pettiness. So we were transformed, at least a little, slowly, and with difficulty. But we were.

Candidate Smith later told me of something that happened in church quite against his will. During the passing of the peace, directly before the communion liturgy, he found himself face-to-face with candidate Jones (not a surprise—we were a small church!). Instead of frowning or turning away, he reached out his hand. "I couldn't believe I did that," he said. "But if there's anyplace where we should be friends, it's right there, before the Lord's Supper."

It was a slow transformation, not a miraculous reconciliation. After the election some folks drifted away even more, never returning to their leadership posts in the parish. They've not joined other churches, they're just in the ether-like netherworld of not-quite-in-my church (what's the joke about the

Baptist stranded on the desert island who built two churches—one was his, one was the one he used to go to?). I'm sure the scars remain for the active political participants. But everyone else realized we were a people of prayer, not politics. They continued reaching out to those who weren't around as much anymore, trying to lure them back. The church has even gained some new members since I left, which suggests a health and vitality that were never lost, only threatened. One has come by way of one of my prayer ladies, a widow, who's got a new boyfriend she's bringing to church. She even sits with him *in a new place*, out of her accustomed seat on the second row (it must be love). The church survived and will continue to. The "credit," such as it is, goes not to my successor, the new young whippersnapper pastor being kept in line. It goes to the prayer ladies who're helping him mind his Bible and reminding him to come to prayer meetin'. As long as there are those churches it always will.

DEAN B. McINTYRE

Dean B. McIntyre is the Director of Music Resources at the General Board of Discipleship in Nashville, Tennessee, a position that includes responsibility for development of musical and worship resources, planning and leading field events related to music and worship, continued development and expansion of GBOD's music website, and the MethodistMusicians email listserv. In addition, he chairs the United Methodist Church's study of worship and music in the denomination for the 2004-2008 quadrennium. Dr. McIntyre has published works for organ, hand-bells, and adult and children's choirs with a number of publishers, and has authored *Hymns for the Revised Common Lectionary*. He is a member of ASCAP and a Life Member of The Fellowship of United Methodists in Music and Worship Arts.

HE IS NOT YET WHAT GOD WILL HAVE HIM TO BE

Justin was just a toddler when I first met him. He was obviously bright and eager to learn. When I went to that church as full-time music director, one of the first things I did was to start a choir for the youngest children—those who were ages four, five, and in kindergarten. I named them the Joyful Noise choir. Their parents and the congregation were thrilled and I always led them myself each week, refusing the suggestion that I farm out that responsibility to a high school student. We played games, folded hands and prayed before eating our snacks, threw balls and jumped rope in the church gym, and always sang songs that we knew and learned new ones, too. About once every two months the Joyful Noise choir would stand on the center chancel steps and sing in worship.

Justin was still three years old when his mother told me he was begging her to let him join the choir. His big sister, Julie, was one of my better singers in the choir for grades 1-3, and she had taught Justin many of the songs they had learned and sung in church. I told Justin's mother to bring him for a couple of rehearsals and we'd see how it went. As it turned out, Justin learned the songs before anyone else. He sang all the right words, and mostly on pitch. He was never disruptive or a behavior problem, he was never late, and he never missed a rehearsal.

One rehearsal day Justin stayed home from his one-morning-a-week Mothers' Day Out daycare at the church because he was sick. By 2:00 he had had a miraculous recovery and was campaigning his mother to take him to

35

choir. Against her better judgment, she gave in. As we began to sing I noticed that Justin was not his usual self. Rather than smiling and singing with great delight, he only sat quietly in his chair. I asked him if something was wrong and he moaned, "My tummy hurts." As I walked him toward the church office to call his mother, he began to throw up. We stopped in the bathroom and I cleaned him up as best I could and we eventually made it to the office and placed the call.

One day as we played in the church gym, Justin ran up to me holding one of the red playground balls. He greeted me with his usual yell, "Hey, Dean!" I asked him what he was doing with that ball and he just shrugged his shoulders, still tightly holding it. I showed him how to bounce the ball once with both hands and then catch it. After he tried a couple of times, he was able to do it. We moved on to bouncing with one hand and catching it, and eventually to actually dribbling the ball with one hand as basketball players do. I demonstrated to Justin how to bounce the ball in rhythm as I sang one of our favorite choir songs, "I Am a Promise." For the rest of the play time that day, that is what he practiced on his own, as he sang "I am a promise. I am a possibility. I am a promise with a capital P. I am a great big bundle of potentiality." That night he greeted his father's arrival home from work with a demonstration of his newly acquired ball bouncing prowess as he sang that children's song by Bill and Gloria Gaither.

As Justin grew, he remained part of the music ministry of that church, moving successively through the various children's and youth choirs, playing handbells, participating in the musicals, the choir tours, singing and playing at the local nursing homes, and caroling for shut-ins. When he was in fifth or sixth grade he became a real helper, assisting me with filing music and setting up and tearing down handbells through the week. And on days when I worked with the youngest children, he helped me in the gym and with preparing and serving their snacks. He took piano lessons and played trombone in the junior high and high school bands, and used both skills at various times in the church. In his high school years, he became somewhat occupied with studies, employment, football and track, and girls, but he remained active and faithful in music at church.

During the fifteen years I served that congregation, I watched Justin grow from a toddler into a strong, intelligent, talented leader. During his senior year he led his high school football team as quarterback to a state championship. He also distinguished himself as a member of the school's debate team and band. Upon graduation he was offered scholarships—both athletic and academic—so that he had a choice of which school to attend and what program to pursue. Following college, he entered training to become an officer in the U.S. Army. Between his commissioning as an officer and his first duty assignment, he returned home to marry his high school girlfriend. It was a great gift for me to be invited to return to play the organ for their wedding, an honor and privilege I had to turn down because of previous commitments.

During Justin's post-high school years we talked only a few times, always by telephone. I would answer the phone and hear the familiar, "Hey, Dean!" and I instantly recognized Justin's voice. We never exchanged letters or emails, other than a Christmas card with a short personal note. Whenever we talked, Justin always recalled some event from the church choir years that made us both laugh. Only once, in a Christmas card, he told me of his feelings during those growing up years, how he so loved the singing, the music, the fun, the experiences, and all of the opportunities given to him in choir, and he thanked me. It was the kind of card and message that one keeps in a desk drawer, to be pulled out, opened, read and re-read in future years.

Last year I had a telephone call from a friend in that church informing me that Justin had been injured by an IED—improvised explosive device—while leading a mission in northern Iraq. Two of the soldiers he commanded had been killed in the explosion, but Justin's wounds were not life-threatening, although he might lose a leg. I was desperate for information on his progress and kept in touch with his parents by email. He did not lose the leg, and eventually came home for a period of recovery.

While at home I managed to reach him by telephone. I wanted to know about him, his prospects, his recovery, and how he was doing, and he wanted to know about me, my job, my travels, and what I was doing. The conversation eventually came to a point where I asked him what he remembered of the explosion. He couldn't really remember it, but vividly remembered waking up to incredibly excruciating pain. Over a period of weeks he was treated and moved to different medical facilities. As he progressed from treatment to rehabilitation, the pain remained but at diminishing levels. He is still in rehabilitation but will make a full recovery.

Justin told me a remarkable thing: in between his cries of pain and agonized outbursts following the explosion, he sang songs—sometimes hymns he had memorized over his years in worship, sometimes choruses from church camp, sometimes anthems from youth choir. But he said the ones he sang the most were the ones he first learned to sing in the Joyful Noise choir. He said that they somehow helped him get through the pain. He didn't know if it was simply a means of distracting himself from the pain or if he was actually deriving strength and comfort from the songs. But over and over he would sing them, sometimes silently to himself, sometimes quietly under his breath and into his pillow. And the first song that he sang and the song he most often sang during those first days of semi-consciousness following the explosion was "I am a promise. I am a possibility. I am a promise with a capital P. I am a great big bundle of potentiality .... I can go anywhere that God wants me to go. I can do anything that God wants me to do ...."

Justin has returned to active duty, now behind a desk in the United States rather than in a truck or armored vehicle in Iraq. He plans to leave the military and return to graduate school. He is singing in the choir at the installation chapel where he is stationed. His future is, indeed, a promise.

I don't know much about music as a transforming agent. Oh, I don't doubt it as such, but I don't really have much experience with it. However, I have many years of experience—personal and anecdotal—with music as an agent in formation, and without formation there can be no transformation.

I think of the many agents active in the formation of Justin as a person and as a leader. Probably most important were his parents and his genetic makeup. Undoubtedly there were school and Sunday School teachers, pastors, coaches, and, thank God, choir directors. There were friends, teammates, employers, sweethearts, and, of course, television, movies, radio, and books. A human being is the product of many factors.

I cannot know what part all of those factors played in making Justin the leader he is today. I do, however, know that music played a crucial role. Music was perhaps the first call Justin heard from God, a call to come and learn and serve the church. Through music Justin learned discipline early in his life. He learned that people count on him to do what he says he will do and that he must honor his commitments. He learned the joys of fellowship and the satisfaction of group effort. He learned both how to take direction and how to offer leadership. He learned how to constantly seek after excellence and improvement. He learned that service—to God and to others—is a worthy life's goal. He learned deep and abiding truths of the Christian faith, and as he grew in wisdom and stature, so too he grew in his experience of God's presence in his life. In all of these lessons, it was the words and music of the hymns and songs that he had sung that allowed Justin to be influenced and formed in his faith. And ultimately it was his musically-informed faith that allowed Justin to call upon the promises of God's comfort, peace, and healing that we so often hear about in church but less often experience.

Justin's near-death experience will prove to be one more agent of his formation and perhaps his transformation. Justin is not yet what God will have him to be. God is still transforming him for future service. Thanks be to God for the gift of music and its capacity to form and transform. And thanks be to God for those who are called and privileged to encourage and nurture that transformation.

ROLAND RINK

Roland Rink is the coordinator for The Upper Room of the work on the African continent. In the next few years he hopes to give a voice to Africans using a variety of media, be it print or oral, to tell their faith stories; stories that need to be told; stories the world waits to hear. One utopian dream he cherishes is that all people, especially young adults, discover early on in their lives what God has planned for them.

He has diplomas in telecommunications, which still come in useful in the work of Africa Upper Room Ministries. He is married, and has two daughters.

The Walk to Emmaus and the Spiritual Exercises of St. Ignatius of Loyola have been important formative events in his spiritual life.

After 57 years, Roland still lives and works in Johannesburg, South Africa, the city and country of his birth. He is passionate about music and enjoys playing and watching sports of all descriptions. He enjoys fly-fishing when time allows.

AFRICA: DAILY APPOINTMENTS WITH GOD

And all of us, with unveiled faces, seeing the glory of the Lord as though reflected in a mirror, are being transformed into the same image from one degree of glory to another; for this comes from the Lord, the Spirit. (2 Cor 3:18)

In an attempt to capture thoughts on transformation from a leadership perspective, I have found it increasingly necessary to differentiate the corporate from the personal. Hereunder follows an account of some Africa Upper Room Ministries (AURM) projects and events that have been significant in terms of being agents of transformation.

Corporate

In recounting some of the stories of transformation that have become a part of the history and fabric of AURM, my hope and prayers are that the end result will be that they will be a source of encouragement, motivation and hope for those who are currently in leadership positions as well as those who are destined to become leaders in the future.

It has been my privilege to lead Africa Upper Room Ministries since 2001. A calling born in 1994 during a visit to Nashville for Emmaus meetings has become the African continental office of Upper Room Ministries. Since our inception in 2001 history and experience as Africa Upper Room Ministries (AURM) the word transformation has come to mean:

The divine and mysterious change that occurs when the seemingly ordinary, the "old fashioned" and mundane, undergoes a metamorphosis, and is changed into something completely different—something new, something that almost always is useful and fulfills a need for all concerned parties in a new and creative way.

In this regard, it has been absolutely vital to have a clear and succinct vision and calling as an organization. Over time the calling and vision of AURM has been distilled to the following statement:

Affording every African the opportunity to spend time with God each day.

The Upper Room Daily Devotional Guide

This small magazine, which has been distributed for over 70 years is a global brand in every sense of the word. It is distributed to 100 countries and translated into more than 40 languages. The pages contain the heartfelt faith stories of men and women from around the world. Each devotion is less than 200 words long and employs simple, yet effective words to describe and trace the hand of God working in the lives of the writers. Many people remember and describe the magazine as being "the daily devotional my grandmother used to read."

It is this same magazine "that my grandmother used to read" that has in the past six years begun to play a small, yet important part in the transformation of the lives of Africans who today, by reading the magazine, follow the daily simple, yet vital disciplines of reading Scripture, prayer, and meditation. It is this same magazine that allows AURM to begin to fulfill its calling.

Today in many African countries, the Upper Room is contextualized, printed, and distributed in new and innovative ways, and most important, in the mother tongue of the reader or listener.

The African English edition of the Upper Room magazine is outwardly not unlike most of the other editions around the world. However, the magazine is contextualized for Africans by Africans who strip away words such as "snow on the backyard fence" (it's safe to say that most Africans have little or no concept of snow!).

The magazine is printed locally at Salty Print in Cape Town, a Methodist inner city mission printing works. The regular and rapidly growing printing work has resulted in Salty Print's employing more people, many of whom were previously unemployed. Also important, it allows Salty Print the opportunity to respond to their vision statement: Transforming paper, people, and places. AURM thus acts as an agent for transformation in the lives of yet another group of people.

The magazine also acts as a vehicle whereby Africans can tell their own faith stories. African devotions are becoming more commonplace in the magazine due to the running of many more writer workshops around the continent. The workshops assist prospective writers in the art of telling their personal faith stories in less than 200 words. Readers outside of Africa are being informed and transformed from this telling of African stories. What a surprise! An African has the same desires, joys, challenges, and issues as the rest of the world!

One of the ways in which the African edition of the magazine has been of benefit to people, and has even transformed other editions of the magazine, has a lot to do with the cultural influence and perspective of the African way of life. Africans by nature are almost always family and community based. By way of explanation, the African word "Ubuntu" means, "I am because we are." No individual is an island. They almost always operate in the context of a community. It was therefore not surprising that after the first few editions of The Upper Room, Africans suggested weekly questions at the back of the magazine for use by their families and groups in their regular weekly class meetings. Traditionally the magazine has been seen as a personal resource. Today many editions carry the questions for group use. The "old magazine my granny used to read" has been transformed from an individual resource into a community resource.

The burgeoning print figures for the African magazine effectively depict the hunger of Africans for good quality spiritual resources. They also confirm yet another transformation. 2001: 6000 copies printed; 2007: 143000 copies printed. Another image is that of Africans waiting for their handout; literally standing in line, waiting with a hand outstretched. (Previously, almost all copies of the magazine were simply given away free of charge.) Today this image is changed, as Africans are now encouraged to make a financial contribution, however small, towards the printing of another copy of the magazine. This has had a transforming effect on the people who use the magazine. It has increased the self esteem of many Africans who realize that they can afford to pay for the magazine whilst at the same time giving a value to the magazine. This financial support has positively transformed AURM's financial statements, which has allowed AURM the freedom to attend to the new challenges that are constantly appearing, in addition to reducing the annual amount needed from the Nashville head office to support the work. With time, the financial independence of AURM will allow Nashville to focus on other areas in need of financial support.

It is fair to say that in the next few years, AURM will be moving through a transforming cycle that will take it from dependence to independence, and finally on to an interdependence with both its headquarters as well as its suppliers and subscriber base.

The Radio

Distribution of virtually any item is one of the most costly and taxing challenges facing any organization in the African context. How does one effectively, regularly, and cost efficiently reach the individual, the person situated in the deepest, most rural parts of Africa and fulfill even their most basic spiritual needs? Clearly, the publication, printing and continental distribution of a bimonthly Christian magazine did not stand a chance of succeeding in fulfilling the original calling in this regard.

The answer was audaciously simple, yet within a short passage of time has proven to be extremely effective. The answer lay in the imaginative use of seemingly "old technology" in the form of radio broadcasts.

Use of radio transmissions by Christian broadcasters around Africa has, in many ways, transformed the African distribution challenge into new and exciting opportunities to reach millions more people. Since the initial pilot broadcasts in 2006, *The Upper Room Devotional* has been translated and broadcast to millions of Africans around the continent in languages they fully understand. Each and every day, a broadcast of the *Devotional* in the Zulu language has the potential to reach over 9 million Zulu speaking people in their mother tongue in Kwa Zulu Natal, South Africa! A highly cost effective method of distribution. The use of radio also lends itself well to the African context in that Africans traditionally have always relied upon the spoken rather than the written word for their history as well as their communal and

personal communications. Important stories in the life of the family have traditionally been passed down from father to son, mother to daughter orally.

Currently the Upper Room is broadcast in the French, Swahili, and Zulu
languages on a regular basis in many African countries. More and more
African based Christian radio stations are requesting the CDs containing the
translated 365 devotions for a full year of broadcasts. Our distribution of the
Daily Devotional on the African continent has thus been transformed by the
use of an almost forgotten technology. Countries such as Chad, Kenya,
Cameroon, Rwanda and Benin have become new recipients of the magazine
in oral form.

The radio edition of the *Devotional* guide today fills the airwaves, the
homes, and the lives of Africans for five minutes each day in previously
undreamt of places. Today, we dare to believe that lives all over Africa are
being transformed by the power of Holy Spirit through these broadcasts. Our
old methodologies and traditional ways of thinking regarding magazine distribution in Africa have forever been transformed.

Mail-Order Catalogs

In June 2005 AURM was granted the opportunity to distribute all Upper Room
and Discipleship Resources books in Africa. As previously mentioned, distribution is a serious challenge for AURM in Africa. The question facing AURM was
simple: "How does one market the wonderful Christian book resources newly
available to all Africans irrespective of where they were geographically located
without embarking along the restrictive, slow and extremely costly path of
opening or supplying retail sales outlets around the continent?"

Again, the answer was to revisit old and trusted methods. The use of mail
order catalogs has long been a method used by many organizations to allow
rural folk the opportunity to acquire items not readily available in the small
local community stores that serve them. In June 2006, the very first AURM
mail order catalog was published.

By using mail order catalogs, AURM believes that it is acting as a transformational agent in the lives of a great number of people. Those in rural
communities, who do not have the means or the facilities of transportation
to large urban shopping malls, now have the same choices as consumers living in the cities and adjacent urban metropolitan areas. Again, our vision

of affording every African the opportunity to spend time with God each day was being achieved.

In keeping with the ethos of AURM, no book is sold for more than Rand 100 (approximately $12). In fact, many books are sold for around R30 ($4). This aggressive pricing structure has not endeared AURM to the local chains of Christian book stores. It would appear that profit may have become a far more compelling motive for many of these organizations than the need to disseminate the Christian message.

In the near future AURM intends to print and publish UR/DR titles in small quantities, using the latest print-on-demand technology of its printing partners.

In faith, we believe that by offering quality resources to Africans, more especially the clergy who are so poorly paid and are in such dire need of new resources to assist their ministries, via the pages of a simple mail order catalog, we are assisting in transforming lives and Christian communities. At the very least, we're offering some modicum of hope and respite for those who seek a closer walk with Christ.

The Super Project

From the very outset, it was apparent that AURM needed a marketing team if it was to be in any way successful in achieving its goal and calling. AURM staff began thinking about with whom and how this marketing initiative would take shape. It was abundantly clear that this could be a very costly exercise with little or no guarantee of success.

For no apparent reason, the word "supernumery" suddenly came to mind. (A word meaning exceeding a certain number, in this instance, years of service). It somehow seemed so logical. AURM should approach retired clergy to form the nucleus of this new sales and marketing team. Not only did they have incredibly good relationships with their communities, but they also had relationships with many other clergy from various denominations. With due haste, we invited them to join us on the journey. Today AURM has five retired clergymen scattered around South Africa who market and promote the use of *The Upper Room Daily Devotional Magazine* in their communities. Without doubt there has been a transformation in the lives of these faithful servants of the Lord. As one of them so bluntly, yet eloquently, put it, "I thought that I was useless to the kingdom within the context of my retirement, but with the Super Project I have realized that I am still useful to the Lord."

Each member of the Super team receives a small stipend each month as well as a commission for the sale of each magazine. The inflow of this much needed additional finance assists these "fathers of the church" to have a better quality of retirement, keeps them in touch with their faith communities, and in most instances, gives them a whole new purpose and meaning.

The utilization once again of the "old" has meant that the Upper Room magazine is read in many parts of South Africa previously only dreamt of. *Note: AURM did not deliberately set out along the Super Project path with any idea or goal of being an agent for transformation. Unwittingly, and because of the whole hearted support of the people involved, AURM has been able to assist to transform the life of retired prayer warriors.*

Once again, the renewal and transformation has come about by the simple act of renewing enthusiasm for tried and tested implements. In this case, retired clergy.

Moses & Me

I am always heartened and encouraged to read the story of Moses' calling. One gains the distinct impression of a "reluctant leader." "I'm not a good speaker, so why choose me for public speeches?" I am definitely not a leader.

The litany of excuses to avoid the responsibilities of leadership can be extensive and imaginative. I suspect that the story of Moses, however, rings true for many people chosen to leadership positions, both inside and outside church. It does for me.

Nonetheless, deep within the souls of leaders, one strongly suspects that our loving God had this purpose for their lives, long before they were born. A sliver of what Wesley termed "Prevenient Grace" perhaps? Sometimes, when the pressures of leadership mount, that fact is about all that leaders have left to cling to.

In times of anxiety and conflict, when confronted by taxing leadership challenges, it is reassuring and comforting for me retrace these thoughts. It is good to remember that ultimately, before accepting the position and being transformed into a leader, I prayed, sought guidance, and tried mightily to discern the voice of God. Oft times, that still small voice competes with loud and brash voices, both internal and external. In my experience, the ongoing exercise of discernment has played a vital, overarching role in almost all decision-making, both corporate and personal; in fact, it is difficult for me to entirely divorce transformation from discernment. I fail to fully understand how leadership in any form can take place without discernment. Yet, sadly, too often as we survey the condition of the world, it is apparent that global leaders possess a distinct lack of discernment. It is clear that they have agendas other than those that will benefit and transform all of humanity. The infamous "hooks" of power, personal glory or pride, and the love of money seem to hold sway.

As I look back over the past few years, I become aware of the gentle, persistent transformation that has taken place in my own life, made possible by the transforming Spirit of a God, who continues to love us, impediments, failings, and all.

Upper Room Libraries

Many who hunger to further their knowledge of the man Jesus; who are intrigued to learn more about the history of the Christian faith; who yearn to deepen their knowledge about the life of present and past leaders in the Christian faith, have simply no means or facilities whereby to acquire the resources needed. As AURM discovered more and more places of need for good quality Christian printed resources within Africa, the idea of libraries was born.

As an organization that is deeply committed to community, AURM has initiated the formation of "Upper Room Libraries" all over South Africa. We placed advertisements in the local church newspaper asking churches for written submissions to become an Upper Room Library. We initially received seven applications. Word has spread, and today we have 14 libraries dotted around the countryside. Most are in low income areas. All receive regular additions to their library from AURM. These books are obtained from the Nashville head office at no cost to AURM, save for the shipping of the books.

One of the challenges faced by AURM was to transform the traditional way people viewed libraries. We simply did not have the means to create a formal library. What we were proposing was a modest shelf of books that would grow over the years, we hope, into many shelves. Perhaps, with time, even a whole room.

A simple one-page document accompanies the first supply of books to each new library. In that one page is all the relevant methodology to begin the library: the rules and items to be concerned about; and the structure and format. In this way we hope to foster a growing circle of resource centers.

Our prayer is that seekers will continue to make use of the Upper Room Library facilities. AURM is providing the resources that will transform people, their families, and perhaps their countries. In the long-term vision, AURM hopes to establish these "islands of Christian resources" all over the continent of Africa.

In conclusion, it has been my privilege and life experience as a South African to have seen a country and its people transformed from being racially divided into a country living together as a fully inclusive democratic society. Out of this experience, one fact is clear: Genuine transformation almost always has to do with two words: risk and freedom. There seem to be invisible yet tangible links between risk, freedom, and transformation.

One needs to revisit the freedom that Spirit gives, the resultant boldness in decision-making that this freedom generates. In truth, how can we not risk watching the plans that God has slowly unfold; both in our personal lives, and in the work we are called to do?

I would encourage anyone who is in leadership, or anyone who is about to enter the realms of leadership, to earnestly seek the freedom that only God can give. Take the risk that our Loving God has only the best intentions for your life, and be transformed as a leader in this process. Allow the One who counts every hair on your head to speak your name and transform and radically change your life forever.

I would like to dedicate this chapter to the leadership team of the GBOD. It is as a result of their visionary leadership and support that the African project God has placed before us continues to thrive grow into exciting and challenging new avenues of mission.

A poem that has been a guide and inspiration for me over many years, sums it all up:

To laugh is to risk appearing the fool.
To weep is to risk appearing sentimental.
To reach out is to risk involvement.

To expose feelings is to risk exposing your true self.

To place your ideas and dreams before the crowd is to risk their love.

To love is to risk being loved in return.

To live is to risk dying.

To hope is to risk despair.

To try is to risk failure.

But the greatest hazard in life is to risk nothing.

The one who risks nothing does nothing, and has nothing –and finally is nothing.

They may avoid sufferings and sorrow,

But they simply cannot learn, feel, change, grow or love.

Chained by their certitude, they are slaves, they have forfeited freedom.

Only those who risk are free! (author unknown)

We go forward!

JAMES C. HOWELL

James C. Howell has been Senior Pastor of Myers Park United Methodist Church in Charlotte, NC, since 2003. A native of Columbia, SC, he earned a Ph.D. in Biblical Theology from Duke University.

His writings include frequent columns and articles in journals like *Christian Century*, and he has published twelve books, the most recent being *The Beatitudes for Today*, and *The Life We Claim: The Apostles' Creed* – and he is now putting the finishing touches on two more books, *The Will of God*, and *Conversations with St. Francis*, to be published in 2008.

Dr. Howell is Adjunct Professor of Preaching at Duke University, and serves on many boards and agencies for his denomination, and in the community, including the Community Building Initiative.

He is married to Lisa and they have three children: Sarah, Grace, and Noah.

"WHAT IS YOUR LEADERSHIP STYLE?"

What is your leadership style?" The question caught me off guard, and left me a bit tongue-tied before a group of younger clergy interviewing me, the veteran, somebody who'd been around plenty long enough to be able to speak articulately about his leadership style. My mind raced through the admittedly paltry number of books I'd read on the subject, or back to the even smaller number of workshops I'd sat through on the subject. As popular as the theme of "leadership" has become, somehow the subject has never captured my fancy. Yes, I lead, and I suppose I lead effectively enough that people inquire from time to time "How do you do it?" But I am never quite sure how to talk about it.

Ron Heifetz declares that it is shrewd to "lead with questions," and he's entirely correct. I'm always asking questions, but not so much as a management technique. I just wonder about things and have never known any better than simply to voice any and every question my mind hatches. My father assures me I practiced the Heifetz leadership style when I was four, or seven, or thirteen-years-old.

Jim Collins informs us that to move "from good to great," the leader need not have personal charisma. I think he's right, although something in me resists slotting myself in that non-charisma category. Perhaps that something is my vanity. While a big personality with charm and clout can prove to be a chimera for a company, or Church, I am left wondering about the singular leaders who galvanized stunning movements in the history of the Church whose personalities were unforgettable, striking, irresistibly compelling:

Martin Luther, Martin Luther King, Francis of Assisi, Mother Teresa, John Chrysostom, Paul, and a holy host of others, joined by, I should imagine, even Jesus himself.

As much as churches try to learn from corporate leadership models, I suspect that, at the end of the day, the shape, the style, the mood of the ordained pastor can (and must!) differ in fundamental ways. I think William Faulkner's eloquent description in *The Sound and the Fury* of the minister of the Compson family maid, Dilsey. He was "a meager figure, hunched over upon itself like that of one long immured in striving with the implacable earth . . . . He was like a worn small rock whelmed by the successive waves of his voice. With his body he seemed to feed the voice that, succubus like, had fleshed its teeth in him. And the congregation seemed to watch with its own eyes while the voice consumed him, until he was nothing and they were nothing and there was not even a voice but instead their hearts were speaking to one another in chanting measures beyond the need for words." This preacher's attitude was that of "a serene, tortured crucifix that transcended its shabbiness and insignificance and made it of no moment." All clergy near this zenith of leadership incandescence will (thankfully) always seem to be square pegs in the round holes of corporate leadership techniques.

The secrets to my leadership? Beyond perhaps not getting too overwrought about which leadership tactics I am deploying? I can think of dozens, including such mundane habits as writings lots of thank you notes, being ultra-organized, and recruiting the next people I will hire even when we aren't looking for anybody yet. But what I wound up talking about when I was quizzed that day were two things, seemingly trivial, and a little bit embarrassing to talk about. But here they are.

First. I think if I am able to lead, a few observers have volunteered the opinion that it is because people look at me and think, "Now there's a guy who really believes what he's talking about." That feels like a chunk of braggadocio, but it's not. I don't think people look at me and think "He's perfect, he's flawless, he never doubts, he is ultra-tight with the Almighty, he never veers from pristine holiness." But I *do* think they believe I believe in the stuff I talk about and am trying to urge them to get involved with.

My hunch is that the Church is unique in this leadership essential. Couldn't you sell Fords, and then turn around and sell Chevrolets? or make money for Bank of America but then head up a university? Certainly, in the business world you have to "believe in" your product, you have to sell whole-heartedly, you understand the need for coherence between the talk and what is delivered. But isn't there always room for (and even need for) BS? Harry Frankfurt wrote that the essence of *Bullshit* (the title of his philosophy book of extraordinary insight) is a total lack of concern of truth. The BSer simply wants to talk you into something or another, and will say or do anything to lure you in. But belief is our business in the Church, and truth is everything in theology.

The business leadership gurus acknowledge that it is the primary role of the CEO to keep the organization focused on the vision; but somehow the theological vision of the truth of the universe is fundamentally of another species from a corporate strategy to sell the best tires. So, if the pastor really believes, leadership can happen. Probably if the people out there didn't like me, or if I somehow didn't appear to be intelligent or well-read, or if there were signs of belief being a thin veneer over a hollow life, the effect would surely be diminished. How delicate is this? The minister has to allow her faith to be on display without strutting it out or creating the circus atmosphere in which the Church is all about this star in the middle with the amazing act on the flying trapeze.

The pastoral leader's first and last thought is: it's not about me. Karl Barth summarized his gargantuan theological project with a single image: the Matthias von Grünewald painting of the crucifixion which is the centerpiece of the Isenheim altar. John the Baptist stands just to Jesus' left, holding a book in his left hand, but with his right hand he is pointing to Jesus, a long, bony index finger cocked toward the dying Jesus. Barth's ambition was "to be that finger." The pastoral leader believes, and merely points, but points urgently and decidedly.

So now rather smoothly we can slide into the second leadership secret that is hardly novel. *(Note: My wife says that if I lose my job I could succeed marvelously as a tour guide. I have actually hauled groups of people on pilgrimages through the Middle East and Europe, and my family has in the same way been trucked to countless places of historic and cultural interest. Always I prepare assiduously in advance, know lots of intriguing facts about the obvious sightseeing venues, but I also nose out some obscurities sure to titillate the fancy of any traveler. I do this with considerable glee, always in the "Hurry, come, see the most amazing thing just at the top of this flight of craggy steps," or "Just give me one*

more hour in this museum and I will show you a treasure you'll never forget.")
To me, the effective leader in Church life is nothing more than a docent. Once
upon a time, Churches were galleries, filled with mosaics, frescoes, illumi-
nated books, shining communion ware, stations of the cross, stained glass,
massive arches, and crypts that defy the imagination. Churches still are galleries, at least in the imagination. What does the effective leader do? We want
people to come, to look, to let their jaws drop in stunned wonder at the story
of our faith, at the sparkling lives of saints, at the inconceivably life-trans-
forming possibilities for being in mission and being a small part of the
adventure of the ages.

No matter how a particular congregation is organized, no matter what
the optimal strategy is in this place to unleash the workers out into the vine-
yards, no matter the posture of hands-on involvement or in-the-background
enabling the leader suspects is the wisest course at this time, the leader main-
tains that docent feel, continually, and in every possible setting, to direct people's attention to the treasures of the Church, to urge them to keep moving,
to do whatever they do with their minds fixed on the stories, the creeds, the
liturgy, the songs, the practices of the Church that dazzle, and give us every
good chance of going somewhere meaningfully integrated into the dawning
of the Kingdom of God.

But is this really a "leadership style"? We hope so . . . and we have seen it
in more circumstances than we remember to thank God for. I was "led" to
study Old Testament in graduate school largely because of a single professor,
Father Roland E. Murphy. He was a noted, much admired scholar, of course;
but his students will never forget his raging, passionate zeal for those books
near the middle of the Bible: Job, Psalms, Proverbs, Ecclesiastes. We do not
remember this or that point he made; but the fire in his eyes, the volume of
his voice, and the way he simply cocked the open Bible were sufficient
exhibits of a man who loved the words on the page, and you couldn't wait to
probe them when you were alone—and then to open the book and rage in
front of somebody else so the contagion would infect them as well.

One of the young associate pastors with whom I had the delight of working showed up at our parish, fresh out of seminary, determined to herd two
thousand people rather unwillingly to oppose the death penalty, to welcome
gays into the Church, and perhaps even to dismantle the military machine of
the United States along the way: not political liberalism, but a deadly serious

read of the gospel and its implications for today. His approach wasn't slick or well-calculated, and actually dozens in our parish were angrily annoyed by him. An older business executive offered to send him to some management school and to a speech coach, which would certainly smooth out the rough edges. Another warned me, "You'd better rein in that new associate." I told them both we'd ruin him if we did. When his time on our staff had ended, a respectable number of arch-conservatives one by one dropped by my office to declare that they missed him, and that he had compelled them to rethink quite a few things. All he had going for him was quite enough: he really believed.

A few years later, another young associate landed in a different parish with me. She sprinted up and down the halls, late for appointments, hair on fire—and in a pretty genteel, culturally elevated kind of place. A few voiced concern about her professionalism, or time management. But she was generally rushing in or out of the building because her heart was clearly out of the building, over across the railroad tracks, with the poor, whom she rather oddly didn't think of as charity cases but as friends, not as objects for our pity but as fellow siblings in the family of God. She could not tell you her leadership style, and most leadership gurus would want to send her off to a workshop or three. But gradually people started rushing around behind her, next to her, showing up late for meetings, hair on fire, spending more and more time out of the building, befriending former charity cases. She was a believer, and it was never about her. She was like a tour guide, grabbing anybody who would come and pointing to the next work of art.

One of those works of art was actually painted by the most surprising of leaders. Our Church is a major supporter of a ministry in the city that works with the homeless. Someone got the brilliant idea to cultivate the talents hidden in the homeless, many of whom turned out to be painters. So they painted, and had an art exhibit. My wife and I wanted to go—but should we drag our twelve-year-old son, who's not at all fond of art or exhibits of much of any kind? Come on, let's go—and he pouted a bit but got in the car. He warmed up when he saw they had chocolate chip cookies, and then we found ourselves standing before a series of intriguing paintings you'd be tempted to call "kitsch." His eyes were drawn to the corniest one of all, Jesus in that ultra-familiar pose, kneeling in Gethsemane. The price was a mere $40. He'd stumbled on a masterpiece, he believed, "Dad, this is the best one in here, and it costs only about a tenth of that one over there that's ugly. Can we buy it?" At about that moment, the artist himself appeared out of nowhere. Big talker, hilarious, boasting of his painting prowess. This Jesus was his favorite (naturally). The canvas? Some velvet he found lying on the ground. The frame? "I found that in the dumpster around the corner." He signed it, talked (at length) about his life, hugged my son—and my wife and I went home with a budding art connoisseur in the back seat with his prize possession.

Oh, how were we led to go to that art show? It was the associate pastor with her hair on fire who mentioned it to us, and we were inclined to believe she's led us somewhere good because we'd had another good associate friend whom nobody could rein in, and because we'd had a teacher who danced as he taught. Leadership that works, that believes, that points to the velvet Jesus framed by some wood saved from the trash heap: that's a style of leadership we'll take whenever we can get it.

REV. YOUNG JIN CHO

Young Jin Cho was born in Korea and graduated from the Methodist Theological Seminary in Seoul, Korea, where he received a Th.B. and a Th.M. He came to the United States in 1979 and continued his studies at Wesley Theological Seminary in Washington, D.C. (M.Div. and D.Min.). He was ordained in the East Annual Conference of the Korean Methodist Church in 1977 and transferred to the Virginia Conference in 1983. He was the senior pastor of the Korean United Methodist Church of Greater Washington (KUMCGW) in McLean, VA for 22 years and now serves as the District Superintendent of the Arlington District.

During his tenure at KUMCGW, the church went through three building projects and developed and implemented the Five-Year Long Range Plan four times, and this church has grown to be one of the most vital congregations in the Virginia conference. Throughout his ministry, Dr. Cho has envisioned the church driven by the vision of Christ.

In addition to his ministry at KUMCGW, he has served the church and the community in various capacities as the president of the Korean Wesley Foundation, president of Partner's Church Association for the renewal of the Korean United Methodist Church, the Virginia Conference Board of Ordained Ministry, and the Commission on Ethnic Minority Local Church Concerns. Dr. Cho received the Denman Evangelism Award in 1991.

He and his wife, Kiok, (Deacon in Full Connection) have two daughters, Grace and Sophia, and one son, Chris.

FOLLOWING THE VISION OF CHRIST

Young Jin, why do you think you have to go back to Korea?"

"I think it's the right thing to do for the churches in Korea," I answered.

Dr. Pyke paused, then said, "Why don't you open yourself to God's guidance? If God needs you in Africa, God will lead you to Africa. If God needs you in China, God will send you to China. Isn't it better to be open to obey God's guidance wherever God leads you? I think this church seems to need you. Please pray about it and follow God's guidance."

It was early in 1983. I was in the Doctor of Ministry program at Wesley Theological Seminary while helping a Korean Church in Washington D.C. on the side. The church had recently purchased ground with a small building in McLean, Virginia, and was preparing to add an addition. Planning to join the Virginia Annual Conference, the church was looking for a new pastor in cooperation with the district superintendent of Arlington. Some of the church leaders asked if I was interested in being appointed to this church, but my answer was "no." My plan was to return to Korea as soon as my studies in the United States were finished. But they persisted in asking me to reconsider.

As a result, I visited Dr. James Pyke, professor of Missions and World Religions at Wesley Theological Seminary, for counsel. Listening to my situation, Dr. Pyke advised me to be open to God's guidance. While singing verses from a Korean hymn, "Lord, we will go wherever you say," I felt God leading me to accept the call from the Korean United Methodist Church of Greater Washington (KUMCGW). That was the beginning of my ministry in the United States. My membership was transferred from the Korean Methodist Church to the Virginia Annual Conference, and I began to serve KUMCGW. Then in 2005, following 22 years of service there, I was appointed to the ministry of district superintendent to the Arlington District.

Finally, A Dream Come True . . . But Then?

The first task given me was leading the congregation through the first phase of a building project. KUMCGW was the first Korean church in the Washington, D.C. area. It began in 1951 as a gathering place to pray for the war in homeland Korea. Once, this church had more than 300 worship attendants each Sunday, but at the time I was appointed, attendance had dropped to around 100. The church had experienced painful splits three times in her history, and the congregation was without hope and confidence in the future. But here we were, building a new sanctuary.

By the grace of God and the dedication of its leaders we finished phase one of the building project on time and within budget. A sanctuary with seating capacity for 200 and six classrooms in the lower level was built. The congregation could finally worship at 11AM, not at 2PM, and cook and eat Korean food, especially kimchee, freely and joyfully. We had a great celebration filled with joy and gratitude to God.

But a question began to surface in my mind and the mind of other leaders. Finally, the dream the congregation had dreamed for over 30 years had come true. Now, where were we to go from here? With this building, what kind of church were we going to be? What ministries were we going to launch? What would be our next step?

At that time, I had the chance to attend "Twelve Keys to an Effective Church" seminar led by Kennon Callahan. I was deeply moved and touched by his leadership and learned the importance of God's vision for the church. During a family retreat in 1984, I shared what I had learned at Callahan's seminar. Our leadership got excited and decided to organize a long range planning committee. We began the process of discerning God's vision for our church.

This beginning became a very important step in my ministry and in the history of KUMCGW. We studied five areas of ministry and developed a plan guided by prayer and discernment: worship/fellowship, mission/evangelism, education, facility and finance.

Based on projections of future growth, we planned to double the present facility size. Strengthening second-generation ministry was primary to this plan because they were our hope and future. From 1986 to 1990, this vision guided KUMCGW, and the church began to grow slowly, but steadily.

Another Challenge

By the end of 1990, average Sunday attendance had grown to over 400. I saw my own life become busier and began to see the need for change in my ministry. I was attending more meetings rather than visiting members as I used to. I began to see the limits of my style of ministry and felt something needed to be done soon. Then I came across an article in a Christian newspaper. It said, "When a church grows and experiences change, the pastor too will be changed. If not, the pastor will easily become a bottleneck." It was an awakening moment for me. I did not want to be a bottleneck for KUMCGW. What was it I had to change? What was the future direction of KUMCGW ? What did the Lord want to change in me?

I turned my eyes outward for help. I began to check out seminars on pastoral leadership. I attended many, including the Willow Creek Leadership Summit, Frazer Memorial UMC seminar, Ginghamsburg UMC, Large Membership Church Conference, etc. Some conferences I attended with my staff and laity, others alone. And through these seminars, I picked up many ideas as to what direction we would need to take to remain a faithful and effective church.

During these years of searching and learning, the church developed its second Five-Year Long-Range Plan (1993-1997). The focus of this plan was on inward growth. We planned to consolidate the foundation on which growth had occurred. KUMCGW introduced the TBC program that was developed in Korea. The TBC (Total Bible Curriculum) is a two-year study program that covers Old and New Testament and church history. In response to an appeal to build a new sanctuary grounded in the Word of God, more than 100 people registered for this program and journeyed through it for two years. The Lord used the TBC program as a means of turning the church around. There was a transformation in the spiritual climate of the church, and many members joined subsequent programs like DISCIPLE Bible Study and Spiritual Growth classes. The second Long Range Plan also emphasized the importance of prayer. For a year all small groups (Wesleyan Class Meetings) gathered around prayer, and I gave emphasis to the prayer life in my sermon series.

In addition to inward growth, the second Long-Range Plan took on another building project to accommodate the growing need for additional space. The church planned to build a new sanctuary and administrative building. It was roughly a two and a half million dollar project. Some of the members expressed concern for this plan. They thought the cost was too high, that the church lacked the financial resources to see it through. In response, many members felt the need for a spiritual revival in addressing the challenges being faced. They began to pray for such a revival.

How Earnestly Do You Pray?

It happened during a planning meeting in 1997. One of the participants asked me a question: "During this year we learned many things about prayer. Pastor Cho preached on prayer, and all small groups studied about prayer. But I have a question about the prayer life of our pastors. How long and earnestly do you pray?" The person who asked this was known for being critical. I was not happy about this blunt question. I said to myself, "Lord, do I have to disclose my prayer life to others? I am doing my best. You know my spiritual life."

But after that day, I could not forget the question: "How long and earnestly do you pray?" It bothered me a lot. I began to feel the need for more prayer in my heart. I decided to begin early morning prayer in the tradition of the Korean church. Every morning I went to church at 6AM and knelt down before the Lord. Gradually, I came to see my spiritual life more clearly. One morning I could not control the tears streaming from my eyes. The Lord graciously helped me to see the real picture of my spiritual life. I confessed, "Lord, I preached to the congregation to pray hard, but I did not pray hard. When some of the members asked me to pray for them, I did not pray faithfully and earnestly for their requests. I did not pray longer, deeper, and harder. I repent of my laziness in my prayer life."

God woke me up by using the comment of a critical person. This experience became another turning point in my spiritual journey and ministry. Soon the church started early morning prayer meetings daily (except

Sundays). The Lord blessed KUMCGW such that the church continued to grow spiritually, numerically, and financially even in the midst of its building project. The building plan finished without any serious problems.

The Second Reformation

In 1998 KUMCGW prepared its third Five-Year Long Range Plan. For the first time the plan did not have a building program. The church continued to grow, but KUMCGW had no room to expand. She was already land-locked. To prepare for this plan some members of the Long-Range Planning Committee and I attended the Saddleback Church seminar. We gained many insights on what constituted a healthy church. The lessons learned during the seminar provided a basis for developing this next plan.

The major goal of the third Long-Range Plan (1998-2002) was developing lay ministry under the theme "Arise and Shine." (Isa 60:1) The laity of KUMCGW had great potential for advancing God's Kingdom. If we buried these talents, we would become irresponsible and lazy servants before the Lord. We discerned that joining the Second Reformation movement was the way KUMCGW should take. Today many Christian leaders are calling the rediscovery of lay ministry the Second Reformation. While the first Reformation handed the Bible to the laity, the Second Reformation is the movement handing ministry over to the laity. Keeping this urgency in mind, we discerned three major directions: Developing lay ministry, restructuring the church to vitalize lay ministry and renewing small groups. In my 22 years of ministry at KUMCGW, this period has been the most transforming.

The team concept replaced committees for lay ministry, and a Council on Lay Ministry Development was formed. Annually, $20,000 was budgeted as scholarship support to help laity attend leadership/training seminars as a part of raising laity leadership within KUMCGW. All ministry teams were grouped into six areas: worship/praise ministry, nurturing/caring ministry, witnessing/outreach ministry, ministry for rising generations, ministry of administration and small group ministry. It was a challenging task to restructure the church, but with prayerful discernment, the task force did a great job. More than 40 lay ministry teams were organized that began to serve the Lord and people in need.

During this period many volunteer mission teams began to share the

Good News of Jesus Christ overseas. Year after year the mission field expanded from Mexico to Bangladesh, China to Tanzania. Long-term mission projects were planned and launched. A mission policy pursuing a balance between foreign and domestic, word and deed, and financial support and hands-on work was developed and adopted by the church.

Change was not always joyful. KUMCGW went through its share of agonizing moments, and I faced my share of criticism. About seven years ago, following up on the third Five-Year Long-Range Plan, we began a process for renewing small group ministries. This plan was adopted by the Church Conference, and small group ministry teams and staff pastors prepared for this renewal plan for over a year. We first trained small group leaders and piloted five small groups for a year under the new small group format. At its conclusion we received positive responses from all pilot groups and decided to expand the new format to the entire congregation. This renewal plan was aimed at the transformation of small groups from fellowship groups to disciple-making groups. New small groups would meet at least twice a month, and the congregation could choose what small group to belong to. In the past, members were assigned to small groups according to their residential area.

Though we prepared this process thoughtfully and cautiously, criticism and opposition began to spread among church members. *Why is Pastor Cho asking us to meet twice a month in today's busy society? Isn't it enough to meet once a month? Pastor Cho was influenced by a small group seminar and is trying to implement it without considering our situation.* One long time member came to me and said, "Rev. Cho, this plan is splitting the congregation. I decided not to join a new small group. Please honor my choice." I was deeply disappointed and frustrated.

On the Sunday the congregation was scheduled to choose their small groups and commit to this renewal process, I went to church early in the morning to kneel down before the Lord. My heart was full of worries, anxieties, and frustrations. There was no peace in my mind. I prayed to God, "Lord, have mercy on this church and on me. As you know and see, we have been struggling with the renewal of small group ministries. There is much opposition. Lord, what shall I do? Help this church and me. We need to move on." I knelt before the altar area and prayed and waited in silence.

After a while, I heard soft and comforting words in my heart. "This church is not yours, but mine." The moment I heard this voice, I was relieved of all anxieties and worries. "Yes, Lord. This church is yours. Not mine. I will leave the future of this church in your hands. If you allow us to move on, we will proceed. But if you have a different plan, we will gladly obey your guidance." That Sunday I shared my experience in the sermon and asked the congregation to forgive me if I had pushed too hard. More than 60% of the congregation committed themselves to the new format of small groups. The renewal plan successfully launched that year.

The Journey Continues

In 2003 KUMCGW developed its fourth Five-Year Long-Range Plan with the theme "Transforming People and the World with the Gospel." Its major goals were strengthening evangelism and small group ministry and developing ministry for the rising generation. It also had a plan to launch a second campus. But the Lord had a different plan for me. In 2005 I was called to a different ministry through our bishop. Through prayerful discernment I responded to this call and left KUMCGW to serve as district superintendent of the Arlington District.

I was neither qualified nor prepared for this ministry. During my tenure the average attendance on Sunday worship at KUMCGW had grown from 100 to over 1,000, and the church has become one of the vital and effective churches in the Virginia Annual Conference. My ministry, however, had been limited to one church, and a Korean church at that, for 22 years. I did not know many pastors within the Virginia Conference and had never served an Anglo congregation. In addition, English was not my native tongue. I was reluctant to say "yes" to the bishop, but I did say "yes." It was because I discerned God's guidance in this appointment.

When I left KUMCGW, the Staff-Parish Relations Committee made an important decision. Though worried and anxious for the future of the church, the members agreed they would welcome whomever the Lord sent rather than trying to find a pastor they wanted. I am still very proud of this decision. Through our Lord's guidance and blessing KUMCGW continues to grow as a faithful and effective church under the new leadership.

Restoring the Lordship of Christ in the church is still my prime agenda, and I am continuing to be open to God's guidance to the best of my ability. I believe that any renewal movement or effort to revitalize the church must begin with the vision of our Lord because Christ is the owner of the church; it is still true that the risen Christ is Lord of the church even in the 21st century. What is important in our mission and ministry is not our vision, but Christ's vision. Developing our vision is important, but prayerfully discerning Christ's vision is more important. And true and authentic revival is not a human creation. It is a gift from God for the church. That is the reason we need to pray harder, longer, and deeper. Just saying "hello" to the Lord will not be enough.

I love what Ignatius Loyola said. It serves as a motto for my ministry: "Work as if everything depended on you. Pray as if everything depended on God."

We work very hard as if everything depended on us. But do we also pray hard as if everything depended on God? Our response may well determine the future of God's church in this present age.

DANIEL SHARP

Daniel Sharp is the Pastor of Worship and the Arts at La Jolla Community Church in La Jolla, California. His responsibilities include designing and implementing all worship services. In addition, he serves in several pastoral capacities with the congregation. He is responsible for training the laity in various capacities for worship leadership as well as overseeing all aspects of the music and worship ministry.

A graduate of Wheaton College, Drake University, and the University of Southern California, Dr. Sharp has served congregations in an urban church in Pittsburgh, a suburban church in Lexington, Massachusetts, southern California churches in Newport Beach and La Jolla, as well as a university church in Seattle. He has lead and developed worship in more traditional styles as well as in contemporary and convergent settings. He has been married for 35 years. He and his wife, Nancy, have two grown sons, Jonathan and Andrew.

In addition, he has been involved in writing and producing numerous musical theatre pieces for worship, concerts, and special services. His greatest love is for choral music. He has conducted major works with full symphony of professional players as well as written musicals for children. He has also been actively involved in team teaching a course on the Church Year at the Robert E. Webber Institute of Worship Studies as well as supervising doctoral theses in worship studies. He has published music with Fred Bock Music Company, including the children's Christmas musical, *Three Wee Kings*, as well as with Hope, and Gentry music publishers. His articles have appeared in *Worship Leader*, *The Journal*, *Creator Magazine*, *The Complete Library of Christian Worship*, *NIV Worship Bible*, and *The Worshiping Church Musician's Edition*.

TRANSFORMATIONAL LEADERSHIP THROUGH A CHORAL MUSIC MINISTRY

There are a variety of ways transformation occurs in the lives of those with whom we work in ministry. In the following few pages are some examples of people whose lives have been significantly affected directly or indirectly through a significant choral music ministry in the local church. Through recounting some of these stories, we'll meet people who grew to a deeper understanding of faith in Jesus Christ, learned to deal better with personal stress, progressed in musical ability, grew in relational skills, found useful places to exercise their God-given gifts, took more responsibility in their own lives, and gained a larger vision for what it means to be a follower of Jesus Christ.

We'll see how ballet, study of some classical devotional literature, musical training, theatrical writing, composing music, acting, and other expressions of ministry, all helped to transform people's lives and, in some cases, see changes that continued long after we had moved on to ministry in a different part of the country.

I had often made the comment, and in fact, it was one of the ministry goals we always shared with the choir, that, "Singing in this choir will change your life, your marriage or other relationships, and will help your faith grow like never before." I even had my senior pastor in one church take me to task for the "arrogance" of such a statement. The choir's response was considerably different than his! If singing in worship doesn't connect with the rest of our lives, what is the point? *Transformation is all about connecting faith and*

73

life in the practical application of daily living. It is also an ongoing process of life, sometimes occurring without the participant's knowledge. What we will be describing did not seem at the time that significant to the individuals, and I believe that is key. There are those "Aha" moments to be sure, but more commonly, life is quite ordinary. At the time the opportunities present themselves, they look more like an indistinguishable fork in the road. However, looking back years later, we discover that little turn was a formational block in building faith.

The following is a pattern that has happened in churches in New England, Southern California, and the Pacific Northwest. The impact on people and changed lives was similar in each place, though the cultures and church settings were very different as you might imagine. This is a compilation of the various stories rolled into one.

Karen

We begin with the story of the ubiquitous "New Members" class. Ours was no different from other churches in that every new member filled out a card indicating all kinds of personal information including skills or talents they might have to share with the larger body of Christ. As I looked through the cards a week or two later, I noticed one person, Karen, had put "ballet" on her card. There was nothing else other than her name, "ballet," and a phone number. Our church was not really into dance of any sort. Though the Bible talked about and described dancing before the Lord, we were a little more cautious.

Later that same year as we prepared for Holy Week, I had programmed the choral piece by Craig Courtney, "Thy Will Be Done." As I was working on the service, I was struck by its particularly descriptive and dramatic nature. I thought, "This is a special service so we'll have a little more latitude for creativity. *Let's take a calculated risk.* I wonder if that 'ballet' person might be able to work something out with this piece." So I decided to give her a call.

I found the card and dialed the number. I was stunned at the response on the other end of the line. "Hello, this is the Boston Ballet. How may I help you?" After swallowing hard, I mumbled out, "Is Karen there?" I wasn't sure if she was an administrator or what. The response came back, "She's with the Bolshoi Ballet rehearsing *Swan Lake* now, but I'll have her call you when she has a break." It turned out, Karen was the *prima donna* of the Boston Ballet!

She called me back and we talked about the idea. She had never done anything quite like this combining mime and ballet. I gave her a tape of the music and she went to work. With the senior pastor's keen interest in what her attire might be, she brought several choices from her wardrobe. After about ten seconds of watching her interpretation of the piece, he was fine. *Our taking a calculated risk gave her a chance to do something truly different than anything she had done before.* That Maundy Thursday service was one of my highlights of ministry. When she finished and we finished the piece, there was a full twenty seconds of stunned silence and thought throughout the 1,000 people in the congregation. We had just seen and heard an interpretation of the crucifixion that we had never before even imagined. Karen's comment later was, "I didn't know I had a gift that could be used in ministry." It was a transforming moment for her and for our whole congregation.

Betty

Every choir has its unique personality and each singer adds to that color. In one particular choir, Betty shared frequently during our prayer times. It seemed that there was a crisis most every week. These were not manufactured times of stress. There was a difficult situation at work; a car broke down; a child got sick; the furnace broke. It just appeared she lived in a "Job-like" world. We did what we could and took offerings to help her with some of the difficult situations. And of course, we prayed. A former choir director had been quite volatile in temperament, which produced a fair amount of emotional insecurity in the choir. I think that environment had affected Betty.

Upon my arrival the choir commented on my organization in rehearsal, scheduling, clear expectation and preparation, even disposition, attention to detail, pastoral concern, as well as some of the devotional material we introduced to the choir. The singers received a rehearsal sheet with the details of the entire rehearsal when they arrived. Humor was a part of every rehearsal. Many singers commented that choir was a "safe" place to be. Over the years, Betty mentioned fewer and fewer "crisis" in rehearsals. They just didn't happen as often. In fact, at our going away banquet from that church, she came up to me and commented. "Do you notice how much more 'normal' I've become?" I assured her I did and rejoiced with her in the work Christ was doing in her life.

Giving clear expectations and goals, exhibiting an even disposition in a leader, maintaining a specific spiritual focus on growing in Christ as individuals and as a choir, all contribute to transforming lives of choir members. Betty is a prime example.

Bill

One of the joys of ministering in different churches over the years is that you have opportunity to cultivate friendships in multiple places. It is often a delight to go back years later to a place of previous ministry. Such was the case a few years ago when I went back to a former church to attend a funeral of a previous choir member. One of the parishioners came up to me after the service and struck up a conversation. Bill had not been a choir member ever, but one who was appreciative of our time there. After a hug and exchange of warm greetings, he immediately said, "Do you remember that Maundy Thursday service you did back in 1994?" This was a good 10-12 years after the service. Bill went on to say that the impact of that service changed his view of God! He commented that the experience was so profound in theological depth and emotion, that it changed his life!

What had happened in that service? I did remember that service specifically. We had a television writer in the congregation as well as several professional actors. We talked about some ideas for portraying the last events of Jesus' life in a realistic fashion. The results were some very moving monologues in musical settings that greatly touched Bill's heart. *By letting go of things others can do (better) and through tapping into gifts and skills that various congregational members had,* we were able to create situations where those gifts might bear fruit. It was most gratifying to know that years and years later, those gifts were still bearing fruit long after the writers and actors were done. It reminded be of that passage in Hebrews 11 where it says, "the blood of Abel's faith still speaks . . . ."

Screenwriters

In a similar situation in another church, two of our playwrights experienced so much success at our church, that one of the theatres in the city adopted one of our Christmas productions into their repertoire for the following year. Both of those writers are now successfully employed in Hollywood writing screenplays. One of the joys of this particular congregation was that we had several very successful professional actors in our congregation who worked with some aspiring younger actors. As a result, one of our young "church" actors has gone on to Hollywood to study acting as a career decision.

By providing the freedom and opportunity, we challenged and empowered people to use and further develop their God-given abilities. Their lives continue to grow and mature in the faith. The screenwriters and actors are deeply committed to carrying their faith into the entertainment world in an endeavor to live the gospel in a very secular market.

George

Recently I had the opportunity to touch base with another of the actors. I hadn't seen him for eight years. As we were catching up, he shared with me these exact words, "Dan, singing with you in the choir changed my life. It changed my marriage. You got me back on the right track. I've been working steadily [in musical theatre] for the last three years. I can't thank you enough." Was this something I had done? No, it was Christ working through what we were doing in the ministry in George's life.

I knew George had significant skills both in singing and in acting. With the help of writers, we created situations where people could flourish. I asked questions, helped guide ideas, and taught the meaning of what we were doing as we worked with the various people. We freely sought to integrate daily life into all the aspects of faith. Living our faith never became a distant part of ministry. We expected their faith to be integrated into the rest of their life activity. *We did more than rehearse; we coached to ensure success on the larger scale of life.* We had ample opportunity to model Christian interaction amidst differing opinions and artistic decisions. We learned how to disagree agreeably. We learned to value family and priorities, sometimes learning the hard way. A positive, forward-looking atmosphere of faith helped to provide an environment for safety and for growth and transformation of people.

Karla

Sometimes the transformation in a person is direct and conscious. Such is the case with Karla. When she auditioned for the choir, I discovered that she had sung as a member of a world-renowned professional chorale in Los Angeles. She had heard our choir and was drawn to the "something different" about this group. She made no profession of faith at the audition but freely admitted that she was searching for a closer connection to God. (I always ask the person to describe their relationship with the Lord in their own words, whatever that relationship may or may not be. The idea is to have some idea of where a person is spiritually and also to make clear from the beginning that this is a spiritual and practical ministry.) I told her that we freely talked of and practiced our faith as a choir. Karla immersed herself in the group and eagerly soaked up everything she could.

Since the choir sang multiple morning services, I offered a Sunday school class one of the hours. The singers sat through one of the worship services of their choosing. They would then leave the other services after we had sung. Many chose to attend the choir Sunday school class. Several non-singing spouses also would join us. Karla became a regular. Through her involvement in rehearsals, Sunday school class, and worship services, she committed her life to Christ. In her words, "I became a Christian because of the choir. I was searching and saw something different in them. I now know that it was Jesus Christ living in the lives of the people in the choir." What did we do? *We simply provided spiritual support for her and let the Holy Spirit work in her life.* Transformation occurred in Karla because we made spiritual life and health central to all we did. Music was our vehicle for spiritual formation in the lives of the singers.

Linda

When Linda, who was in her early 20s, came in to my office she was very shy. It was hard for her to even look at me. She had a lovely clear voice, even if somewhat timid. As we talked, it was clear that her past lifestyle had been somewhat "wandering." However, Linda said that she heard the choir sing and wanted to take some steps to get her life back on the right track. She thought the choir might be a good place to begin and she loved to sing. She had grown up in a Christian family, a child of missionary parents. She knew the basics of faith, but had chosen her own path to this point.

During the first couple of years singing in the choir, Linda began to change. She became much more intentional in her walk with the Lord. She made the decision to go on a music mission trip with the choir to Ukraine. Though quiet, she became much more outgoing and adventuresome. Musically she progressed beautifully and gained tremendously in confidence. She began to audition for various solo parts with the choir. Her extremely high tessitura was a marvelous asset to the choir's overall sound. She sang with abandon. She became reliable and responsible. She was always on time and prepared.

A year after we left that church, we got a long letter from her along with a wedding invitation. She decided to go back to school and finish her college music degree in voice. Linda asked if I would write her a letter of recommendation. She was accepted into the vocal performance major program. She also wanted to thank me for helping her to "become the Christian woman God intended her to be." In her words, singing in the choir changed her life both musically and spiritually. She got direction, maturity, and stability in her life.

How did this happen? God was gracious. We challenged the singers to think deeply about the character of God, the ramifications of Jesus' work on the cross, the nature of music in worship. As part of our weekly two and a half hour rehearsals, we regularly worked our way through various portions of Scripture and classic devotional writings (eight-ten minutes of the rehearsal) such as *The Imitation of Christ* (Thomas a Kempis), *The Pursuit of God* (AW Tozer), *Screwtape Letters* (CS Lewis), and such. I taught a choir Sunday school class on the impact of the Church Year on spiritual formation. We also created situations in which Linda's musical gifts could flourish. We worked with her and showed confidence in her ability. *We demonstrated trust in her and believed she could do it. We also placed her in situations where we felt certain she would experience success.* We did not expect too much too soon. We wanted to keep her in situations where she could experience success along the way as the responsibilities increased. And we always cheered along the way.

Martha

Then there is the story of Martha, another 20-something person who came into my office to audition for choir. She had recently moved to the area to be near a parent who was in a health crisis situation. Martha had recently graduated from college with a vocal performance major. Her mother wanted her to continue singing and also joined the choir so they would have something to do together. When Martha began her audition, it was one of those times when in the first five seconds you know you are hearing an astounding voice. Such was the case. The beauty in the whole things was that Martha, at that point, didn't really know how beautiful and natural her voice was. It was a voice made for opera.

There were some musical things that needed some attention and there was also the confidence factor. Singing in front of large crowds of people made her quite nervous and it reflected musically. I worked with her on various musical things as well as poise in singing. One day she asked if she could talk to me about perhaps making opera a career choice. She had several questions regarding a Christian singing in the secular world of opera. I assured her the Lord could use her anywhere and the opera world certainly needed people like her. After some more conversations, she decided to head in that direction. The response from the opera world has been tremendous to say the least. Scholarships and internship programs opened for her. Significant people in the world of opera heard her and talked with her and gave her tremendous encouragement and well as opportunities to sing on a much larger stage and broaden her ministry as a person.

So how did this happen? God allowed our paths to cross for a few years. *During that time we engaged in significant conversations, which resulted in clarity of direction and life changing direction. A transformational leader is tuned to the bigger picture in people's lives and guides them in that direction. He/she shares knowledge, information, and skills.* The practical application of her faith grew by leaps and bounds. We simply worked through the natural situations that arose. We tried to pay attention to what God was doing in our midst.

Bill

There are the stories of a retired teacher who began publishing music with a major choral publisher as a result of some ministry opportunities that developed, a hired professional instrumentalist who came to faith as a result of playing in a Christmas concert, a couple who met in choir and got married, and on and on. But a final story is that of Bill. Bill sang in the choir and was the executive director of a national non-profit organization. He decided he wanted to do something else. In fact he wanted to work with us in the music ministry. He was most gifted and certainly overqualified for the position. But he loved what we were doing and wanted to learn more about worship and music and the relationship between the two. I was involved in teaching in the Robert E. Webber Institute of Worship Studies. Through my correspondence with my students from that school, Bill became more and more intrigued with the relationship between music and worship. Through daily interaction and treating ministry seriously, he found intellectual and spiritual nurture and became hungry for more. I made my personal library available to him and he devoured book after book. We'd have conversations about some of the books and ideas that emerged from them. *Through practicing what I preach and our conversations about such,* he eventually enrolled as a student at the REBIWS. He is in the process of earning a Masters degree in worship studies. His life is undergoing a major transformation through observation of and interaction with his leader.

Conclusion

What kinds of situations occur that encourage these kinds of transformational activity? More often than not, it is the ordinary tasks of music ministry. *The transformational leader has the mindset of a teacher. The teacher is thinking "student involvement in the process" rather than the result of final product.* Music ministry is not about preparing for performance. It is about teaching the *how* and the *why* of faith. As you read, the majority of the most significant times of interaction were spontaneous. The Holy Spirit was at work in our midst. It is clear that the more closely a leader is tuned to the ministry of the Holy Spirit in his or her own life, the more likely he/she will be aware of the opportunities to encourage transformation.

Transformational leadership is a continual challenge, privilege, and delight. Nothing in ministry is more thrilling than to see lives change before our eyes for the building of the kingdom of Christ.

WILLIAM H. WILLIMON

The Reverend Dr. William H. Willimon was elected in July 2004 as Bishop of The United Methodist Church. He leads the 157,000 Methodists and 792 pastors in North Alabama. For twenty years he was Dean of the Chapel and Professor of Christian Ministry at Duke University, Durham, North Carolina.

Dr. Willimon is a graduate of Wofford College (B.A., 1968), Yale Divinity School (M.Div., 1971) and Emory University (S.T.D., 1973). He has served as pastor of churches in Georgia and South Carolina. For four years, beginning in 1976, he served as Assistant Professor of Liturgy and Worship at Duke Divinity School, teaching courses in liturgics and homiletics and served as Director of the Ministerial Course of Study School at Duke, and Presiding Minister in the Divinity School Chapel. When he returned to the parish ministry in 1980, he was Visiting Associate Professor of Liturgy and Worship at Duke for three years. He also serves on the faculties of Birmingham-Southern College as Visiting Distinguished Professor and as Visiting Research Professor at Duke Univeristy Divinity School.

Bishop Willimon has given lectures and taught courses at many pastors' schools and at colleges and universities in the United States, Canada, Europe and Asia. His articles have appeared in many publications including *The Christian Ministry*, *Quarterly Review*, *Liturgy*, *Worship* and *Christianity Today*. He is Editor-at-Large for *The Christian Century*. He has served as Editor and Expositor (with his wife, Patricia) for Abingdon's *International Lesson Annual*. He has written curriculum materials and video for youth, young adults, and adults.

A 2005 study by the Pulpit and Pew Research Center found that Bishop Willimon is the second most widely read author by mainline Protestant pastors. His nearly sixty books have been translated into eight languages and have sold over a million copies.

WHAT IF I'M WRONG?

I believe in transformative leadership. I want to be a transformative leader. I believe that my institution—the United Methodist Church—is in desperate need of transformation, renovation, and rejuvenation. I believe that, in our Conference, we have initiated measures that will accomplish transformation. Yet here is my question: *What if I'm wrong?*

What if our initiatives and efforts to transform are unsuccessful? What if God does not bless our strategies for renewal of a declining part of the body of Christ? What if our decline is irreversible and our only future is either death or life in a greatly diminished and demoralized state? My church has lost about a third of its membership in thirty years and, if my demographic calculations are correct, the loss will increase geometrically in the next decade. I really believe that the reorganization and very different ways of working that are now taking place in my Conference are answers to what ails us. While it is too early to see results, I believe that we shall eventually reap positive results. But what if I'm wrong?

To equip myself for this work I've read dozens of leadership and management books on transformative leadership, both secular and sacred. Among the best of the secular are Jim Collins (*Good to Great*), Ron Heifetz (*Leadership Without Easy Answers*), and Marcus Buckingham (*First Break All the Rules*). The best of the religious are Paul Borden and Bill Easum (two church renewal leaders with many books to their credit). The authors of these books tend to be confident and upbeat—after all, why write the book if you are not convinced that God has shown you a way that works? No management guru I know thinks that indecision and self-doubt, hesitancy and consternation are qualities of an effective transformational leader. Still, what if I'm wrong?

If I'm wrong, and my ideas and programs prove to be ineffective, it will be very sad. It will not only mean that I have personally failed (I was, after all, a campus minister and seminary professor for 25 years, so I can handle failure!). It will mean that my beloved church has failed, at least in that segment of the church that is working and praying for transformation and renewal.

I don't mean to trumpet my own righteousness, but I don't see too many leaders in my church who are attempting to transform. Maintenance of decline is still the order of the day for the majority of our ecclesiastical leaders. An irony is that many of them in my denomination think of themselves as "liberal," or "innovative" but they are progressive only in their theology. When it comes to the institution, it's still management of the status quo. After all, it is the status quo that put them where they are so what's wrong with the status quo?

If my ideas for transformation are wrong, then that's sad because I just don't hear too many ideas, certainly ideas in motion, ideas that are being put into practice, other than my ideas. Most of the initiatives in my Conference have their source and their most persistent implementation in me. I say that not out of pride but with some sadness. I wish that more of us church leaders were busy flooding a moribund system with new ideas. If I'm wrong, then I'm not sure there are lots of counter proposals waiting in the wings to be implemented.

And if I'm wrong and this doesn't work, I know enough of group dynamics to know that my failure will empower and validate all those who are waiting in the wings to proclaim, "See? These big ideas of change didn't work. We were right and the transformationists were wrong. We will never change—we told you so. There. Let that be an end to all this talk of transformation."

And if I'm wrong, it is unlikely that there will be other attempts at transformation because there will be very little left to transform. As I said, I believe we have a window that allows for dramatic intervention on our part but after that time there will be even more precipitous, perhaps completely irreversible decline.

And yet, maybe some of my self-doubts and reservations are an essential component of transformational leadership, or at least specifically Christian transformational leadership. The Christian faith teaches that I am a sinner, after all. My redemption is not finished, not by a long shot. While I like to impute the very best of motives to every action I take, the Christian faith tells me that my actions, even some of the very best of them, are still shot through with sin. I am more self-deceitful than I'll ever fully know.

Admission of my sin, even the sin I don't yet know to be sin, is not self-doubt so much as simple realism. Therefore, when people criticize me or question my motives or the final results, they are not necessarily being obtuse and resistant to change. They may be right. I need to listen to them, carefully and prayerfully consider their criticism, and then be willing to repent—I mean make adjustment to my plans and goals in light of their revealing criticism.

This is a prejudiced Christian statement (the only sort of statement you should expect me to make!) but I would say no one should go out to be a transformative leader who is not a Christian. The person who rises up and proclaims, "I am a visionary, transformative leader, follow me!" is a person who is prone to self-delusion and capable of great wrong. Just to ask, "What if I'm wrong?" may be an essential quality of truly transformational leaders, a gift of having been taught that I am, despite all the management and leadership books that I have read, a sinner.

One more thing. My vocation is transformational leadership *in the body of Christ.* As I read many books on leadership, even the very best of them, I get the impression that transformation is the result of savvy technique, well applied principles of management, and hard human work. All of that can be true, to a degree, but none of it is true without prior acknowledgement that real transformation is a work of God. Grace. Alas, too much that passes for transformation today is simply that which technique can deliver. What if our goal is not simply a strengthened United Methodist church but nothing less than "a new heaven and a new earth"? Only God is able to kill and make alive. What the church is called by God to do only God can do.

So this implies that, if I'm right, it is because God takes my pitiful offering of inept leadership and somehow makes it right, somehow weaves my poor efforts into divine work. If I'm right, then it's as a gift, not as a result of my hard work or astute insights. If I'm right, then it's because somehow, despite my resistance, God has miraculously taken my life and enabled it to be congruent with God's purposes that are always larger and more important than my life or even my church. There is also the reassurance that many of my leadership failures are due to God. God simply did not need nor want what I offered. This is a great mystery but is an everyday experience of living in a world that is God's and not mine.

One of the greatest compliments ever paid me was by a District Superintendent. He told one of our pastors that we wanted to appoint him to a sad little rural congregation in North Alabama. He told the District Superintendent, "That church is dead! It's been dying for years. I can't go there!"

The District Superintendent replied, "Well, I'll tell the bishop that's your reaction to this. But let me warn you, this bishop really believes in the resurrection of the body about as much as anybody I've met. So to say to him, 'that church is dead' means nothing to him. He considers death an opportunity to validate his theology."

I hope what the District Superintendent said about me is true. I really do.

It is this gifted, gracious, frighteningly-dependent-upon-God quality that is missing from much of our thought about transformative leadership. We live in a time in which we are conditioned to think and to live as if Jesus did not rise from the dead, as if it doesn't matter whether God is or isn't. Therefore Christians must discipline ourselves to live and to lead in such a way that the question, "What if I'm wrong?" can only be answered by a crucified and risen Savior who is determined to get the world that he wants.

So finally, I don't know if I'm right or if I'm wrong in my efforts to lead renewal in United Methodism. But finally, God knows. As Luther once said, "When we were right, God laughed at our righteousness." Whether I'm right or whether I'm wrong, God is going to have to take my right and my wrong and weave it into God's purposes. At the end of the day, no matter how many things I get right, the things that I'm trying to do will need a God who loves to raise the dead and to create something out of nothing if they are to bear good fruit. At the end of the day, I'll need a God who loves to forgive sinners, or all my right is but silly self-delusion and all my wrong stays that way.

Fortunately, Scripture tells of a Savior who was crucified, in great part, because he just loves to be with sinners. Thank God.

VALERIE BRIDGEMAN DAVIS

The Rev. Valerie Bridgeman Davis, Ph.D., is associate professor of Hebrew Bible/Homiletics and Worship at Memphis Theological Seminary. She is the founding director of the seminary's The Return Beat: Syncopating Theology and the Arts Institute. She serves as general editor and consultant for the United Methodist Church's Africana Worship project. In addition, she leads the "Tribe," a collective of young artists who use their art as a spiritual discipline in service to ending violence among young adults, especially gang members. She is an acclaimed published poet.

Dr. Bridgeman Davis graduated from Baylor University with a Ph.D. in biblical studies (Hebrew Bible concentration) and secondary studies in ethics.

A Sermon
for My Mother

Bernice O'Neal McKinney Bridgeman had a lasting impact on everyone she touched. She was as a schoolteacher, church mother, and community activist in central Alabama. My mother recruited people to walk for March of Dimes back when the sheets literally had dime slots to fill in. She sewed for neighborhood groups, makings outfits for entire wedding parties—including the men's tuxedoes. She planned and organized Vacation Bible School at her home church, Pine Grove Baptist Church in Odena.

What I most remember about her was her encouraging support, not just for us—her family—but for everyone in the area. Bernice's integrity was a force unto itself. An incident between my mother and me remains my most vivid example of integrity. I had accompanied my mother to the local convenient store. Once there, standing at the counter, she realized that $5 was missing from her purse. She accused me, right there in front of the store owner, of taking the money. I was humiliated. We arrived home and I stomped into the room I shared with my sisters. About 15 minutes later, my mother called me. "Come, go with me," she said. I didn't want to go, but couldn't refuse. We got back into the car and drove back to the store, the place of my great humiliation. I was dumbfounded. "Get out the car and come with me," my mother insisted. Sullen, I entered the store again. She asked to see Mr. Casey, the man in front of whom she had accused me. When he came, she said, "I accused Valerie of stealing in front of you a few minutes ago. I was wrong. I found the $5 stuck in a side pocket when I got home." Then turning to me she said, "Valerie, I should never have made such an accusation, especially not in front of someone else. Will you forgive me?" I was all of ten-years-old, and an adult, my mother no less, was asking for my forgiveness. I am many years from that incident, but it became a guiding moment in my parenting years. Treat your children with respect. Never make accusations, especially in front of people.

When Bernice began to suffer the effects of memory problems and Parkinson's disease, people who had experienced her fierce care and concern came to her aid. Like many self-sufficient people, she didn't take too kindly to being looked after. She had always been the helper, not the one needing help. But as the years grew short, she submitted to the care of her kin and her friends.

About six weeks before my mother died, she was alert and recognizing her children and grandchildren. We had moved our parents the year before to Georgia to be near family members who would better take care of them. Mama's dry wit cracked us up as we laughed at her straight-faced comments. I took her for a ride in her wheelchair and she chided my driving abilities. I read to her the familiar Psalms and prayed with her. I stroked her hair and sang to her. She sang along, the words of long-ago learned hymns still coming through the fog. It was Easter weekend, 2002.

I returned to my Texas home with a sad heart. Although my mother was alert, I was sure her time was short. Then, the call came from my youngest sister, Gwendolyn. Mama had a stroke; she has sepsis; doctors unsure of the prognosis. I started lobbying for hospice care. For as long as I could remember my mother had insisted that she did not want to be kept alive artificially, including being fed through a tube. As hard as it would be to let her go, it would be harder to watch her suffer the indignities of aggressive treatments that would prolong her agony. Within a week, the doctor noted that there was nothing else to do medically, and she was moved to a hospice facility.

I decided to drive to Georgia from Texas. I told my husband that I needed the time to myself to think and to pray. I needed to prepare to see my mother in a helpless state. Fifteen years before, my mother had asked me to preach her funeral, if I were alive when she died. At the time, I told her I would make no such promise, that I couldn't know what emotional state I would be in when that time came. But on the way to Georgia, a sermon started formulated in my head. "She served her generation well" was the title. I remembered the Scripture connected with the phrase, Acts 13. By the time I arrived at the hospice, I knew I would be able to preach my mother's funeral. Peace took over my emotions and resolve settled into my bones. My mother was going to die. I knew it because I had the sermon for her funeral, and I would have to preach it.

For a week, we gathered around my mother's bed and told stories about growing up as her daughters and about her life. Curled into a fetal position because of the stroke she'd suffered, my mother seemed diminutive and help-less. But that was only the physical sense. Her face was relaxed. She refused all attempts to try to feed her or give her water in her semi-conscious state. "I'm only cooling your tongue and wetting your lips, Mama," I would say before she would part her lips slightly and allow the cool wet sponge on her tongue. When her tongue was cooled, she clamped her lips closed. I found it easy to respect her decision. My mother had decided to die. She believed the faith she had taught us all those years. She believed in the resurrection, in life after life. She had made peace with God and with death. Her peace gave me peace.

On May 7, my youngest sister and I sat by my mother's bed. We were again making each other laugh with tales about our mother. My dad, Robert, walked into the room and kissed my mother. "Honey, I want to kiss you one last time, while the blood is running warm in your veins," he said. We watched, tears forming in our eyes. I asked whether he would stay, but he said one of the nurses said Mama didn't want him there when she died. So, he left. My sister and I moved closer, sensing a shift in the atmosphere. Thirty min-utes later, my mother gasped. We stood. I put my hand on her head; my sis-ter touched her chest. "Mama, was that your last breath?" Gwen asked. Mama took another breath, and died. I looked up at the clock. It was 6:45 p.m. I went to get the nurse to have her pronounced dead. After the nurse con-firmed what we knew, we sang "Heaven Bound," one of my mother's favorite songs. Our family started arriving. We called all the others. I went to my sis-ter's house, and finished writing the sermon. She served her generation, and the generations beyond her, well.

JOHN SAVAGE

John Savage is a senior consultant with The Kilgore Group, LLC and the founder of LEAD (Leadership, Education and Development) Consultants, Inc. He specializes in working with churches, non-profit and business organizations. His expertise is in the fields of listening dynamics, conflict management and resolution, training, and consulting.

Dr. Savage holds four earned degrees: A B.A. in Music from Syracuse University School of Music, an M.A. in Religious Education from Syracuse University, an M.Div. from Colgate Rochester Divinity School and a D.Min. (in the field of psychotherapy) from Colgate Rochester Divinity School.

He has written two books, *The Apathetic and Bored Church Member* and Listening and *Caring Skills*. He has also written numerous articles for *Leadership Magazine*. He has been on the adjunct faculties of Princeton Seminary (8 years), Toronto Theological Seminary (20 years), and is currently adjunct faculty training doctoral students at Seabury Western Seminary.

Dr. Savage has worked with over 40 denominations in Australia, Canada, Taiwan, New Zealand, England, and Scotland. The LEAD system that he founded has taught over 100,000 people in 14 countries. He has created over 30 different training events, many of which have been tailor-made for the client. His specialty is to create a training event that meets the agreed upon well-formed outcome of the client.

Dr. Savage has worked with corporations and other organizations, such as:

IBM, training top executives,

Hewlett Packard training 350 persons in depth listening skills,

Second and third year medical students at Ohio State University Medical
School,

Power utility managers in Australia,

Principals of High Schools,

Nurses in a nursing college,

Top executive in many denominations including, United Methodists,
Southern Baptists, Evangelical Lutheran Church of America,
American Baptists.

He has done original research in the fields of the church drop-out, congregational corporate pain, and just recently on "Spiritual Intelligence."

Leadership Development by the Decade

Introduction

I have spent the last 20 years of my life observing and studying the phenomena of how a belief system gets installed in the human brain. Maybe that is why I pay so much attention to the formation of leadership based on early belief installations in childhood and the teenage years. We know from research that the brain develops rapidly during the preschool years. Thus the person is getting wired for life. When the beliefs are powerfully positive, and life giving, and produce significant rewards, they are anchored deeply into the unconscious and act as life-long drivers and motivators.

This chapter will explore how the formation of those early beliefs motivate and shape the skills and competencies in adult life.

When Hugh Ballou called and asked if I would write a chapter on a person with exceptional leadership skills, the first person I thought of was Charlotte Bougher.

Why Charlotte? Why is she so special? First, she is the music director of Gender Road Christian Church, in Columbus, Ohio. Second, she has done more with the choir(s) than any previous director. Third, and most of all, is beloved by everyone who meets and works with her.

Her first choir rehearsal was exceptional. Never before had I heard of anyone doing this kind of welcome, let alone knowing someone who actually did it.

It was about 7:15 PM—choir starts at 7:30 PM—and 20 choir members file into the room. They are about to meet their new choir director. Charlotte was there before the first person arrived. As each member walked into the room ,she greeted each of them by their first names. They all responded with smiles and a warm response back to her, thinking to themselves, "How did she know who I was?" The choir has long remembered that experience.

How *was* she able to know those choir members when she had never met any of them before? This is what she did. She asked the church secretary for the congregational pictorial directory. She then took the list of names of the choir members that hung on the bulletin board in the choir room, circled each picture and name, and committed to memory the faces and names of each member. Consequently, she has never forgotten one name.

That was the beginning of what has turned into a wonderful choir experience with Charlotte's leadership and relational style. Now the question is, "How did she become such an excellent leader, teacher, and choral director?" This chapter will attempt to answer that question.

I called Charlotte and asked if I could interview her for at least two hours. I had come to know her from many church activities, from sitting with her several times at lunch, and from traveling with her on three choir tours. But because I am a trained listener and interviewer, I thought I would try something different with her by having her tell me about her leadership experiences by the decade. I wanted to find out what happened in each ten-year period of her life and how each decade contributed to the next in developing her leadership style. Therefore, the rest of this chapter is divided into sections—one for each decade of her life.

The First Decade: Forming a Leader in a Young Child

This is how it all started. Lanie, Charlotte's mother, played piano for a studio school and took Charlotte with her. (It should be noted that Charlotte's mother is an exceptional pianist, teacher, and organist, and still accompanies the choir at the age of 85.) It was in this setting that Charlotte started to do something at the age of five that set a leadership pattern for the rest of her life. It all seemed so simple when she told me the way this pattern expanded itself in each of the later decades.

"I would sit out front and learn the dance steps the others were learning, and then I would teach other students the steps," Charlotte said. " I learned quickly and then enjoyed teaching others, including teaching others how to teach." Within five minutes of starting the interview she told me this, then added "My mother made me think I was special. My mother was an encourager. I never heard my mother tell one negative story about me to another person."

This encouragement was the reinforcement for a pattern that was started simply by a child, then picked up sensitively by a mother who gave her permission to perpetuate it. It became the pattern for a lifetime.

When I do these decade interviews I listen for four things: the person's beliefs, values, patterns, and behaviors. In the simple construct of the material above, the pattern built a belief (that she was special), and it perpetuated into her school years. She said, "In fourth grade, my teachers thought I was good at what I did—that I was different and not the norm." She believed what her teachers told her, and this anchored an emotional response in her of feeling good about her abilities and produced its own reward. She valued what she did. That value system is still in place today. She loves to teach others how to perform, and seeing them accomplish their goals is her reward.

This approach to her leadership has led her to be "other" oriented. She does what she does for the sake of the individuals in the group and the group as a whole. Thus, she pays attention to how the other person is doing. She is encouraging of others, particularly a group like the choir. She gets the members of the choir to compliment each other, encourage each other, (She often says, "Now turn to the person next to you and say, 'You're awesome,'" or some other affirming and encouraging thing.) This brings laughter and affirmation to the choir.

The 10-20 Decade: Personal faith Gets Inserted Into the Pattern

"God was always a part of my life," Charlotte said. "My parents were youth leaders and they modeled for me how to love children, and taught me how to be open to others in helping them." And then something happened that gave Charlotte grit—the ability to stick to something when she did not like it.

Her mother put pressure on her to take piano lessons. "It was the thing I disliked . . . it was like a wall I had to get through." The struggle of learning how to go through experiences she did not like gave her a strategy she would employ when encountering other difficult times in her life. Only later in this article will you really know how the power of the ability to manage personal difficulties added to her leadership style and tenacity.

As a result of gritting it out and struggling with her piano lessons, she has become an excellent pianist. The end result of this struggle is that she has become very motivated to teach others.

Probably one of the more guiding beliefs that became installed in these teen years was a statement she said to herself during these teenage years that had power and influence in it. She stated, "I do not fail at the same thing twice!" In back of that statement is her intense interest in learning what she does wrong and correcting it quickly. The belief of not failing twice became attached to another belief: "If I see it, I can do it by modeling what I see." This belief grew from her early childhood practice of sitting and watching children dance, thus allowing her to learn the steps through observation. Because Charlotte has surrounded herself with people of excellence, she has been able to model "best behaviors" and accept them as part of herself.

In this interview some of her thoughts came in rapidly-fired comments that followed one after the other. Like, "I have to be a leader, not a follower." "I *need* to be productive . . . I *have* to be productive." She then said that those years (from ages 10-19) "contain the quality that makes us who we are."

At this point in the interview, I began to realize that all of these beliefs and values began to mold even more intensely the leader that was in the making.

Charlotte's self-talk about not failing twice became very powerful during these teenage years. That is because what she said to herself is what she started to become. With these initial beliefs, she now had to deal with another personal struggle.

These teenage years were not always easy for her. She had developed a mild condition of ADHD that made her exceedingly active. This also made it difficult for her to develop close friendships that lasted more than a few years. Charlotte told me that making friends back then was problematic because she always wanted to be the leader, and that did not work out with all the groups she was in. Thus, she moved from group to group. That has changed, and she learned to overcome her difficulties and turn them into her strengths.

I want to share how these beliefs and values turned into life patterns in the next decades of her life.

The 20-30 Decade: The Years of Discovery, "I Can Make a Difference."

In her 20s, Charlotte began to develop excellent choral leadership among adults and youth. These became groups of people that she could teach, and one of her common comments over and over in the interview was, "I can make a difference. I motivate myself. I did music well and easily, and God's call was on my life." She added, "I was called to preach—my life is the message and my preaching was done through music and the people I work with." She graduated from college summa cum laude, third from the top of 120 students, and was voted outstanding senior of the year by the faculty. It was her belief of "making a difference" that gave her motivation and purpose. This led into the next decade where she shifted her concern to a very personal approach. People became more important than the context in which she taught them.

30–40 Decade: Teaching People, Not Content

In her 30s and on into her 40s, Charlotte discovered the phenomena that many leaders experience as they developed through the years; that is, how to work with a large, diverse population. She accepted the position of music director at a local academy for boys, which, after a few years, became co-ed. It was here that she learned to become inclusive in her leadership. The boys and girls came from a large, diverse cultural background. Executives moved to this area from different countries and sent their children to the academy because of its academic excellence. These children represented diverse religious groups, including Christians, Jews, Muslims, and Hindus.

As she came to the boys academy, she discovered that the boys did not sing well. They basically did not like music. It was her job, she said, "to turn that around." She handed them canes and hats and had them dance first, then sing. Remember, one of her guiding beliefs is that "I do not fail at the same thing twice!" The first time with the boys, she had tried just singing. It didn't work because they did not know how. By starting with the dancing this time, she led them into the music. It did not take her long with this second technique to turn these boys into a thriving musical group who put on a song and dance titled, "Puttin' on the Ritz."

In these years, she added a dimension to her leadership, which has become one of her most significant long-term leadership abilities. She takes the group the way it is. She said to me, "God leads me to have you do the unbelievable. And we do it." Her ultimate intention with every group she works with is to make it better than she found it. That certainly is true with the groups she is currently working with at Gender Road Christian Church.

Charlotte discovered in her late 30s to mid-40s that, "I can use what I have for either doing right or wrong. It is always a choice. I'm a leader who wants to influence persons to do their best." She also told me, "I work with people, and I work very hard at not letting anyone really know who I like and who I don't." Her approach to her leadership style is that of "modeler." She never forces a person to participate, but invites all. Her goal is not necessarily to have you become a musician so much as to have you feel good about singing.

"My approach to my work," she said, "is to have fun, because fun energizes you, and wakes you up." The choir at GRCC will tell you that they have fun and laugh a lot.

The 40–50 Decade: The Three Keys to Leadership

A key characteristic of an accomplished leader is the ability to continually work with a group of people so that they improve in their relationship with others and in their relationship with God. As Charlotte has matured as a leader in this decade, she said that three things constitute her approach and philosophy of being an excellent leader. (By the way, she would never admit she is an excellent leader. She has a level of humility that is obvious and important to her soft management style.) Here are the three things that she mentioned: Trust, Purpose, and Encouragement. In trying to live out these three things she stated, "I want to see how God works in my life and that of others. I want to align myself with what God wants for me. That is the drive that is in me."

Maybe the most profound little comment that she said to me comes in this little quip. I think it is marvelous: "Have a good morning—against all the odds."

In the last decade or so, Charlotte has dedicated herself to four different things that link up with the leadership concepts above of trust, purpose, and encouragement.

1. Influence change. She is there to make things different; to make it better and healthier and more wholesome. That is the change she seeks.

2. Resolve conflicts. It would be impossible to have a group such as the choir work together if they were fighting with each other. So part of her work is the resolution of conflicts within the group she leads.

3. Make tough calls and difficult decisions. This requires her to make the kinds of decisions that would always be beneficial to the group, even if the group didn't always like it.

4. Know that the leader cannot always make everyone happy. Although Charlotte tries very hard to have everyone like her, she knows that some people will misinterpret her behavior or challenge her ideas.

Because Charlotte is a collaborator, she is always open to feedback when something seems reasonable and possible. She is quick to make adjustments and to take the advice of other people, when appropriate.

The Present Decade: The Years of Maturity

It was while she was in her 50s that Charlotte chose to retire from her teaching and leadership position at the Boys and Girls Academy. As a result, she became available to work for Gender Road Christian Church in Columbus, Ohio. She said, "I had no idea of what was ahead of me after I retired from the Academy. I am here at this church because I am aware that my whole life is an expression of my relationship with God. God loves us, and I am here in this church because I believe this is where God led me."

In these later years, Charlotte wanted to work on building her finest and best character, so she started working on her own behavior. Part of her purpose was to either prepare or repair her own relationships, but also help others do the same.

She has discovered that there are some things that do "bug" her and make it difficult for her to be a leader. The persons with whom she has the most difficulty are persons who are self absorbed or as she put it, "They need to get out of themselves."

Charlotte is now more skilled, more dedicated, and more capable with an incredible number of competencies in her ability to lead a group, whether it is a group of young children, teenagers, or an adult choir. She has developed an excellent small orchestra within the last six months. A year ago it did not exist.

I spoke to a very active church member recently (who is not in the choir) and told him that I was writing this chapter on Charlotte's leadership. He burst into a big smile and said, "She is the best, and we love her." Throughout her life, Charlotte had been able to commit herself to develop levels of excellence both in her musicianship and the leadership of people.

Of all the things that Charlotte told me, I believe the thing that you must remember out of this chapter is this:

1. You must have people trust you, and if that doesn't happen the next two don't matter.

2. You must have a purpose for your life and for those you are leading. And they must be of a common mission.

3. You must encourage people to do their best.

As I reflect on these concepts that Charlotte shared with me, I realize that I see persons in leadership positions who do not do these three behaviors. Can you imagine a person who does not build trust, who does not have a specific purpose for his or her people, and does not encourage anyone?

I hope you've found this material helpful. I am thankful to Charlotte for her gift of leadership and her willingness to share her experiences, her journey, and how each decade of her life contributed to developing the excellent leader she has become.

Footnote: Since the writing of this chapter, Charlotte's Senior Choir at Gender Road Christian Church (Disciples of Christ) has been invited to sing at the World Convention of the Church of Christ in Nashville, TN. The choir has also been invited to sing at the World Advent Choral Festival in Prague, Czech Republic.

THOMAS H. TROEGER

Thomas H. Troeger is the J. Edward and Ruth Cox Lantz Professor of Christian Communication at the Yale Divinity School in New Haven, Connecticut. He began serving in this position July 1, 2005.

From June 1991 through June 2005 he was the Ralph E. and Norma E. Peck Professor of Preaching and Communications at Iliff School of Theology in Denver, Colorado. While at Iliff he established and directed the school's Doctor of Ministry program in homiletics, and served a three-year term as dean of academic affairs.

Ordained in the Presbyterian Church in 1970 and in the Episcopal Church in 1999, he is dually aligned with both traditions. He ministered for seven years as a pastor (1970-1977), and then taught homiletics for fourteen years at Colgate Rochester Divinity School/Bexley Hall before coming to Iliff in 1991.

After ordination as a priest, he became one of the associate clergy of St. John's Episcopal Cathedral in Denver.

Author of more than a dozen books in the fields of preaching and worship and a frequent contributor to journals, he is also a flutist and a poet whose work appears in the hymnals of many denominations. Much of his teaching and scholarship has focused on the function of the imagination in the life of faith. His books include *Imagining a Sermon, Borrowed Light: Hymn Texts, Prayers, And Poems, Ten Strategies for Preaching in a Multi-Media Culture, Preaching while the Church Is under Reconstruction, New Proclamation, Above The Moon Earth Rises: Hymn Texts, Anthems And Poems For A New Creation*, and his most recent work, *Preaching and Worship*. Many contemporary composers set his poetic works as anthems for SABT choirs.

For three years he hosted the *Season of Worship* broadcast for Cokesbury. He has led conferences and lectureships in worship and preaching throughout North America, and in Holland, Australia, Japan, and South Africa.

He has been awarded honorary doctorates by Dickinson College and Virginia Theological Seminary for his work in homiletics, liturgy and hymnody, and a Founders Day Medal by Baker University for distinguished service in theological education.

His hobbies include playing chamber music, cooking, hiking, and cross-country and downhill skiing.

Broccoli, Chocolate, Tigers, Butterflies: Transformational Teaching as Faithfulness to the Creator

After thirty years of teaching homiletics, hymnody, and worship, I no longer say I teach those subjects. Instead, I describe myself as one who teaches preachers, hymn writers, and liturgists. I teach students, not subject matter. At first the distinction may sound suspect. After all, my courses include reading books and handing in assignments. But in fact the distinction transforms my understanding of teaching. If I say I teach a subject to students, then the implication is that there is an objective body of knowledge that I know and they do not, and my task is to get that knowledge into them. They are blank computer screens waiting for me to begin typing in the message: this is what we know and here is the way to do it.

But the nature of the arts that I teach requires that I engage the creative gifts of my students. They are going to be preaching and leading worship Sunday after Sunday, year after year. Often they will be writing or searching for hymns, prayers, and forms of ritual expression that help their congregations come to terms with global complexities, with new realities that the human heart needs to lift to God. The issue is not how well students do in the course, but rather will the course awaken and empower them to sustain the visionary energies that are essential for lively and faithful ministry?

The first thing I tell students is that I am going to teach them what they already know but do not know that they know. Their self perception, often reinforced by their earlier education, blocks this knowledge from view. They see themselves as "uncreative" or "unimaginative" or "unpoetic" or "unmusical" or "unable to speak in public." My task is to transform them by helping them to undo all those self misperceptions that begin with the prefix "un," all those things that entangle and suppress their creative capacities. My starting assumption is that students bring to class profound experiences, insights, and intuitions, and they frequently possess astonishing knowledge about matters of which I am ignorant. All of these elements constitute the juice, the vital intellectual and emotional nutrients that can sustain a life time of creative, visionary ministry.

I have found my teaching is most transformational, that it most engages the creative gifts of students, when I lead by following the Spirit of creativity that suffuses the poetic creation stories in Genesis. There are two different accounts of the creation of humanity in the opening chapters of the Bible, and each of these stories reveals that our capacity to create is built into the nature of how we are made.

The first story tells us that we are made in "the image of God." There are multiple ways of interpreting that famous phrase, but for now I want to focus on just one: to be made in the image of God is to be created to create. When the image of God appears in the first chapter of the first book of the Bible, the only thing we have seen God do is create. Later there will be an abundance of other depictions of God—as liberator, shepherd, bread of life, wind and fire—but the first portrayal of God is God the creator. To bear God's image is to bear the capacity to create.

The second story of the creation of human beings includes God's invitation for us to participate in naming the animals, to be a partner with God in creating the world through the opportunity to speak it into verbal existence. Creativity and partnership: I lead class by following the One who has woven these abilities, these spiritual gifts, into the bio-chemical processes and neuron structure of our brains. We are created to create in partnership with the Spirit whose creativity includes gathering matter into the explosive densities of the big bang and setting loose the processes of evolution that resulted in broccoli, chocolate, tigers, butterflies, cobras, mongooses, and human beings inhabiting this same little watered stone whirling in the immensities of space. We are made in the image of the wildly creative God who did all that! I understand my teaching, my drawing forth the creative gifts of students, as a way of honoring the deep dear core of things from whom the process of the entire universe unfolds and who in the opening chapters of Genesis has said in effect to all of us, "You are able and invited to use the creative gifts I have given you."

Just as the opening chapter of the Bible affirms the human capacity to create, so too, the transformation of students begins when teachers recognize that capacity in their students. Honoring their gifts initiates the process of freeing students from the misperception that they are "uncreative" or "unimaginative" or "unpoetic" or "unmusical" or "unable to speak in public." Teaching becomes transformational leadership as students begin to make connections between their experiences, insights, and intuitions, and the knowledge they possess in other fields of enquiry and expression. Creativity flows from the integrative act of drawing together in new configurations what they already know and expanding the horizon of what they see as they delve into new domains of knowledge.

I have summarized these theological underpinnings of my drawing forth the creative gifts of others in the following hymn text that was commissioned by a church sponsoring a religious arts festival on the theme, "created to create."

The crickets chanting through the night,
the windswept, whistling trees,
the birds that welcome morning light,
the humming, roaring seas
are each assigned the notes they sing
while we make up our part
and fashion God an offering
through our creative art.

The budding wood, the flowered field,
the mountain robed in snow,
the burrow and the nest that shield
the beasts from winds that blow
are from the same inventive mind
that dared to set us free
to probe how nature is designed
and bring new worlds to be.

Created to create, we ask,
O God, before we start
that you will join us in our task
by moving in our heart
so everything that we create,
compose, produce, invent
will help the earth to celebrate
and honor your intent.[1]

The prayer to God that concludes the hymn is crucial to engaging rightly the creative gifts of students. The gift of creativity, like all divine gifts, can be used in distorted and destructive ways, and this includes in sermons, hymns, and worship services. We have only to think of the sad and brutal history of the church's preaching the inferiority of different races, the inequality of men and women, attacks on science and the free exchange of ideas. But the potential for misusing a gift is no excuse for neglecting it. If that were so, then we would have to abandon every gift that God has given us.

Instead of neglecting the holy gift of human creativity, transformational teaching cultivates its critical use. For sermons there are standards of theological integrity, clarity of thought, and rhetorical effectiveness; for hymns there are standards of euphony, metrical precision, and faithful imagination; for liturgies there are standards of structure, spontaneity, and their appropriate balance. And behind all of these is the ultimate theological standard: our prayer that "everything that we create,/compose, produce, invent/will help the earth to celebrate/and honor God's intent."

Sometimes we create at a high level of excellence and sometimes we do not. Critical judgment is integral to the creative act itself. But once again, I have discovered that transformational teaching is not simply a matter of the teacher applying external standards to the evaluation of a student's work. That is only the first step toward a more important and enduring process: namely, developing the ability of students themselves to evaluate what they create throughout their lives. The same teaching that brings forth creativity also cultivates the ability of students to examine what they produce long after the course has ended. Transformational teachers help students learn how to learn from themselves for the rest of their lives. Students become for themselves what their instructors were for them during their brief season in the classroom: partners of the One who in the beginning created the heavens and the earth, agents of the Spirit who sweeps over the deep and engages every receptive heart in the transformation of the world.

Thomas H. Troeger, *Above the Moon Earth Rises: Hymn texts, anthems, and poems for a new creation,* New York: Oxford University Press, 2002, p. 16.

JEFFREY MICKLE

Rev. Jeffrey Mickle is a United Methodist elder in the Virginia Conference. He grew up near Johnstown, Pennsylvania, and graduated from the University of Pittsburgh at Johnstown (B.A., history). He received his M.Div. and Th.M. from the Divinity School at Duke University, where he met his wife, Rev. Deborah Austin, also an elder in Virginia. They have been pastors of churches in Virginia since 1981. Jeff has served the Shenandoah Charge, Aldersgate Church (Alexandria) as associate, Resurrection Church (a church of Philipinos and Anglos), and Belmont Church (Richmond). Jeff and Deborah have two sons, Jonathan and Benjamin.

CROSSING BRIDGES OF RACE AND CLASS IN CONGREGATIONAL TRANSFORMATION

B elmont Church is located in the outer urban ring of Richmond, Virginia. When it was started in 1956, it was in a new suburban community in Chesterfield County. In 1973, Belmont and its neighborhood were annexed into the City of Richmond. It became a "transitional community," and over the next twenty years, the community's demographics moved from predominantly Euro-American and middle class to an African-American majority and lower middle to lower class population. Belmont Church remained a Euro-American congregation, with a shrinking congregation, many driving in from the suburbs and growing older together.

In the Richmond District, the clear trend had been for almost all churches in transitional communities to either close or relocate (sometimes with merger) to the suburbs. It was like a domino effect, with four United Methodist Churches within five miles of Belmont falling to the challenges of being unable to maintain viable ministries in their "changing" communities, within a period of twelve years. Belmont was the next domino in line to fall.

The bishop appointed me to serve this congregation in June, 1994. Shortly after my arrival, my new district superintendent, future bishop Ray Chamberlain, took me out to lunch and shared with me a story about the *kairos* opportunities—how he had tried to do something different and creative at one point in time and it failed; later, when circumstances seemed to be more inviting he tried the same kind of thing and it flourished. His point was that it is important to be patient and to watch for the fullness of time, the *kairos* opportunities, which God creates for us as instruments of the kingdom.

At Belmont, it took years of trust-building, care-giving, friendship-developing, seed-planting, unfruitful attempts, disappointments, and regular signs of encouragement that "there is still a vision for the appointed time . . . . If it seems to tarry; wait for it; it will surely come, it will not delay." (Habakkuk 2:3)

Today, in early 2007, Belmont is a racially diversified congregation, with an average attendance of 140, of which 20-25% are African American and the remainder is Euro-American; we include among our number those who are homeless, many who are impoverished, lower income working class, as well as middle class and upper middle class persons. We are vitally connected with our community, and hundreds of persons in the community look to us as the place where the love of Jesus reaches out to touch their lives, even though they are not yet in attendance at Sunday worship.

The catalysts for the transformation included a couple of *kairos* moments, surrounded by the ins and outs, ups and downs, joys and concerns of everyday life in the body of Christ. What follows is written from my perspective as pastor, but there are many others in the congregation who have been instrumentally involved and who could tell the same story from different perspectives.

The first four years serving Belmont were foundation-laying years. During the first months I visited the congregation in their homes, listened to their stories and to the reasons why Belmont Church was important in their lives. A common theme emerged, first in my mind, later to be articulated in group settings: that God has been at work here for a long time, building up a people of love and hospitality. In other words, we are a people who have been formed to welcome the stranger.

Beginning the first year, and continuing for the next ten years, I led two or three groups of DISCIPLE Bible study. About half of the worshiping congregation participated in these significant spiritual formation events, getting to know me not only as a teacher, but also as a person. The break time with refreshments became significant in relationship-building while the study itself allowed opportunity to develop a sense of common understanding, mission, and vision flowing from the Scriptures and enlivened by the Spirit.

We undertook some capital repair projects that required extra fund-raising and they went well. When the time came to take those capital improvements to the next level with the possible installation of an elevator, some of the financial leaders suggested that we create a long-range planning committee to look at the needs of the church from a more comprehensive perspective, rather than simply moving from one project to the next without an overall plan. This long-range planning committee, sparked by the desire for a church elevator, became the instrument for much more than capital improvements.

After four years of building trust, getting to know people, becoming part of the fellowship, and gaining respect as a pastor, teacher, and administrator by doing what I said I would do, it was now time to look at some significant systemic change. In his commentary, *First and Second Samuel* (Westminster, 1999), Eugene Peterson says of David,

> The text makes clear that the initiative for the anointing of David comes from the elders of Israel. Although anointed to this office early in his life by Samuel, David did not press his claim or use his Hebron-based military supremacy to impose his kingship on the tribes of the north. David knows how to wait. His waiting is not procrastination; it is not indolence. It is poised submissiveness, a not-doing that leaves adequate space and time for God's initiating actions through others. David has been waiting a long time. He has not been unoccupied during the waiting, but neither has he impatiently asserted his own claims or God-given rights. (pp. 156-157, commenting on 2 Samuel 5:1-5)

The long-range planning committee undertook a two-year process of demographic study, small group sharing and listening, congregational surveys, prayer, and Scripture study. Important lay leaders were included as part of the committee, including some who might not be supportive of change. We built a congregational consensus that we would commit ourselves to become a vital outpost for Christ in the community where we had been planted, and we would do what it took to prepare for the next generation of faithful ministry. It boiled down to two components, detailed below: first, people; then, building.

As the long-range planning committee was undertaking its work, we began a second worship service, one designed for seekers, with multi-media, drama, seeker-friendly messages, contemporary music, etc. It was a huge commitment of time and energy on my part, and after a couple of years was becoming a drain on my stamina (read: approaching "burnout"). I told the Staff-Parish Relations Committee that I needed to get some help.

The Finance Committee had to consider our financial resources. It was a stretch to add $1,000 a month for a seminarian. We discussed it, and there were the usual voices of how little we had, but one of the leaders spoke up and said, "We really have no choice. If we want to be here ten years from now, we've got to do this." Heads nodded around the room. We were under way.

In Richmond, there are three seminaries: two predominantly Euro-American and one predominantly African-American. By this time, the long-range planning committee had all the demographic information to demonstrate that our community was more than 50% African-American, while our congregation had only one active African-American member. I said that we should concentrate our search at the African-American seminary at Virginia Union University. There was debate on the committee, but eventually everyone agreed, even if they thought "it would never work," that we should try to hire an African-American seminarian.

We put fliers on the bulletin boards at the seminary, but there was no response. We made personal contact through a Euro-American seminarian (from our church) who was attending Virginia Union, but nothing emerged. We asked our district superintendent if he had any leads from his small group interaction with the seminarians, and he came back with only one name, a senior, who had only one more semester before graduating and looking for a full-time appointment. I despaired that our plan was not working out. This soon-to-be last semester seminarian visited our worship services one Sunday, and I spoke with him, explaining that we were really hoping to get someone who could come and serve as a seminarian for more than just a few months. But, if he wanted to apply we would certainly consider him. He was the only applicant. The committee interviewed Brian Brown, and fell in love immediately. He was God's gift for just this time.

As the year of Jubilee began, on January 1, 2000, Belmont entered our era of an intentional ministry of racial reconciliation. Brian began his part-time work, preaching regularly and leading worship weekly. At the time, we were writing two different sermons for each Sunday, and developing a multi-media power point presentation to accompany one of them. His assistance was a Godsend to me, simply in terms of taking over some of the work load. But it soon became apparent that his presence was much more than that. The people of Belmont bonded with Brian and his family and soon decided that we did not want to lose him when he graduated. We asked the bishop to consider a full-time associate pastorate, which he agreed to. But how to fund it? A special mid-year appeal to raise an additional $24,000 for six months of salary and support was pledged in less than a month. We took it as a sign that God was opening the way for this ministry to continue.

With Brian as a full-time partner in a ministry of racial reconciliation, we could move forward with the "people" component of our long-range plan. He orchestrated an after-school ministry, using the bridges of race that opened doors to local school principals that had been closed when we had approached those same principals a few years earlier for a similar program. As part of the after-school ministry, we required that all participants sing in Belmont's newly organized children's choir which was drawn from the after-school children. That choir would sing once a month. We had 15-20 children in the program, about evenly divided between Euro-Americans and African Americans. The first Sunday when they sang, I looked over the congregation, populated not only by the children but by their families, and it was like a miracle! The vision of a congregation where the walls of race were being broken down, and the unity in Christ was breaking forth emerged before our eyes. Both Brian and I were deeply inspired. A few of those families started attending Belmont even on the Sundays when the choir was not singing, and the presence of African Americans in the congregation slowly began to grow from one person in the late 1990s to four or five families in the early 2000s. Brian stayed for two years as associate, before moving to become the solo pastor at Asbury United Methodist Church, in another section of Richmond.

Rather than break the ties that the Lord had been building, Asbury Church was gracious to enter into an agreement with Belmont so that we would become the Asbury-Belmont Cooperative (ABC) Parish, joined together by a common mission of racial reconciliation. The pastors exchanged pulpits monthly. The congregations planned quarterly fellowship, worship, or mission events. Several DISCIPLE Bible study classes were formed with persons from both congregations participating together weekly.

Belmont was gaining an identity as a church where racial reconciliation was not only being dreamed of, but was actually being lived out.

We partnered with a community organization to facilitate in-depth dialogues about racial history, attitudes, and healing. We organized a group called Reconciliation PALS (Prayer, Action, Learning, Support) that met weekly for about a year, then moved to monthly meetings. This group acts as a place where issues of race are openly discussed, wrestled with, and new understandings and insights emerge. It is a kind of leaven for the entire congregation's journey, though there are many in the congregation who have not participated in the kind of in-depth dialogue that the "leaveners" have. Sermons have given voice to the vision for racial reconciliation and regularly explored scriptural texts through the prism of this ministry. We do not preach "racial reconciliation;" we preach the Gospel, and racial reconciliation is one of the fruits that emerges for our context.

We discovered that God was building bridges between Belmont and some African Americans, mostly middle class. As we began to hear one another's stories, we could see how God was using the experiences from our earlier histories to bring us to this place of joining in a common journey, witnessing to the kingdom's call for racial unity. We have lost some members who did not approve of a stance of advocacy for racial justice and against racial insensitivity. We have lost some financial support as those members left.

The next step in our journey of congregational transformation was across the bridge of class. Beginning small, with the idea of keeping a few groceries on hand for people who drop by needing food, Belmont's food pantry was soon to emerge as a key bridge to serve and welcome persons who faced struggles providing sufficient food for their families.

At Thanksgiving 2004, we were distributing our usual Thanksgiving baskets, and someone called for one at the last minute, after all our food was distributed. One of our new members was standing there when I announced the dilemma. She volunteered to go and buy the groceries and deliver them to the requesting family herself. Here was someone with a heart for ministering to the hungry. Not long after that, I asked her if she would like to be a coordinator for taking our food pantry to another level. She eagerly agreed.

With the help of some faithful long-standing members, and the indispensable energy of some excited new members, we decided to open a food pantry every Friday morning, putting a sign in the front yard, gleaning from area grocery stores, and trying to meet the needs of whoever showed up. We began in January, 2004, and have reached a plateau of serving about 130 families per week with 4-5 bags of nutritious groceries, along with a clothes closet that never seems to run out of good quality used clothing. The food pantry was founded on the principle that the people who came needed more than just physical food. We offered to pray with persons, arranged for Stephen Ministers to be on hand for quality listening, and began each Friday with a time of worship before officially opening the doors. We had asked God to open doors to our community, and God opened the back door where the food pantry is located. Every week there are new people, new seeds, new relationships, new awakenings in grace and faith.

A small group of "fired up" disciples gathered to rework our mission statement, and developed a new one: "Belmont Church is a family of Christ called to be a vital center for community ministry, where people of all races can find passion for Christ and compassion for others." We now sing a version of this every week at worship as a way to re-gather after passing the peace. Expanding the passing the peace and including weekly songs from the African American tradition were important parts of changing the worship service to build a diversified congregation.

In 2005, we began another bridge-building ministry, called Tuesdays Together, designed to invite the Friday morning "congregation" to become more a part of the fellowship of Belmont's existing congregation. On Tuesday evening, we have a fellowship meal, and time for worship, Bible study, children's ministry, and youth ministry. Many persons have come into the Sunday morning worshiping community across the Tuesdays Together bridge.

At first, the class barrier broke down among the Euro-Americans, so we became a congregation of middle class whites, blacks, and poorer whites. Then, the class barrier with African Americans came tumbling down. In the process, the original Belmont family has been transformed, to become much more focused in our identity as agents of God's Kingdom building in our community, as persons who value the opportunity to build friendships with the "other" whom we might have feared just a few years ago, and as witnesses to the power of the Gospel to overcome the dividing wall of hostility and replace it with a community of love, faith, and hope for a new day. We can only imagine the impact on the generation of children growing up at

Belmont who may grow up and move away to discover that most churches are still divided by race, and to wonder what it will be like to think that racial separateness is not the way it's supposed to be, not just in theory but in practice.

Along the way, we finished a major building renovation project (2003-2004), creating new fellowship space to provide room for people to gather before and after worship, as well as to update the building with more modern nursery and restroom facilities. We are beginning the next phase of building, which is to add a community center to house the food pantry, clothes closet, and other shalom-building ministries.

We continue to be blessed by African American partner clergy. Since Brian has left, we have hired the Rev. Barbara Nollie (2002-2004) and the Rev. Gwen Andrews (2004-present) to provide part-time leadership, leading worship every Sunday and preaching regularly, as well as continuing to work with children and youth from the church and community. Both Rev. Nollie and Rev. Andrews are Baptists, there being a very limited pool of United Methodists in our area. Both have been integral to the ongoing integrity of our journey. They have offered their personal stature to the importance of this ministry of racial reconciliation, and allowed Belmont to make a credible witness that we not only have good intentions but are also serious about enacting our intentions.

Instead of the dominoes continuing to fall, God has shown us another way, where the Gospel's message takes hold in a community to transform it from the inside out, building on the foundation of hospitality, Scripture-based vision of God's kingdom, and *kairos* moments that provide the opportunities for us to say "yes" to yet another door that opens in the adventure of being the people of Christ.

Seven Days of Prayer for
The Local Church

Please join tens of thousands of other church leaders as we pray the same seven requests for the future hope of the church.

Sunday – **Passionate Worship** – Lord, we pray that Churches across the globe would have an awesome encounter of worshipping You in Spirit and in truth today (John 4:24).

Monday – **Calling Young People into Ministry** – Lord, we pray that You would raise up laborers for the harvest (Matthew 9:37-39). And, specifically, we ask You to raise up young clergy in America and call them into the ministry of the local Church.

Tuesday – **New Churches** – Lord, we pray that You would raise up new Churches in America in places where there is no vibrant witness for the Gospel right now (Romans 15:20).

Wednesday – **Ministry to the Poor** – Lord, we pray that You would use the local churches to alleviate poverty, stamp out malaria and HIV/AIDS, and minister to the less fortunate and overlooked in the name of Jesus (Matthew 25:40).

Thursday – **Renewed Vitality of the Local Church**– Lord, we pray that You would bring renewed vitality to the local Church (Ezekiel 37) and that You would daily add to Your church through professions of faith (Acts 2:47).

Friday – **Unity** – Lord, we pray for a healthy unity across the community of churches such that the unbelieving world may see and believe in You (John 17:20-21).

Saturday – **The Word** – Lord, we pray that as the Word of God is preached in our church and other local churches tomorrow that You would bear fruit that will last forever (Isaiah 55:10-11).

For a downloadable resource that can be used in your local church setting, go to www.cor.org/catatyst. This resource is provided in an easy to use Word Document and can be adapted to best meet your needs.

B.J. DOHRMANN

B.J. Dohrmann is the founder of IBI Global, hosting the premier Entrepreneur Training and educational products serving the world market (see www.ibglobal.com and www.CEOSpace.BIZ).

Dohrman is the author of *Money Magic, Grow Rich with Diamonds, Living Life as a Super Achiever* and *Perfection CAN Be Had*. He is host of American Dreamers Radio, www.americandreamersradio.com), and the inventor of Super Teaching for public and private schools, one of the first classroom redesign approaches since the 14th Century. Dohrmann lectures on cooperative versus competitive systems in the work place, Super Teaching, and Entrepreneur Curriculum Sequence for K-12 to Upper Education. He is currently working on a series of feature films based upon his life, and on two new books: *Redemption: A Cooperation Manifesto*, and *Digital Diet: A Call for Moderation in Digital Addictions*.

B.J. Dohrmann resides in Madison, Alabama with his wife, Lynn.

STRANGE AND WONDERFUL PLANS

I remember my first day of prison. I left my beloved wife and children in tears, wracked with the pain of betrayal and injustice, and arrived early hoping to make a good impression. That didn't work. In the three-man jail cell built to house only one, I watched a tattooed drug violator unpack my locker. He said, "Boy, Doc is going to be mad you're taking all his space."

He was right. During my first hour of incarceration I watched him and Doc, my new cell mates, steal my watch, my personal belongings, and all the photos I'd brought from home, and I felt alone. In my new home, I was afraid for my personal safety. Nothing prepares you to move from your home to prison. Nothing ever could

Almost ten years earlier, I had sold a multi-million dollar, publicly-traded investment firm to a Midwest attorney. The new owner stopped paying the debenture bond offering and eventually caused an $87,000 investor loss. This gave my childhood friend, who had become a high-ranking attorney and government official, an opportunity he had apparently been waiting for.

While we had both achieved success in our lives, my path had resulted in much greater wealth, and when my former business was taken to court, he used his power to involve me and to defame my character. The stress of ten years of court proceedings and unwarranted harassment got to me and resulted in a charge of contempt—the lowest federal category possible.

The day the jury came back with the verdict on the charge against me, I remember the word like thunder on marble, "Guilty." I remember the mean-spirited stare from my former best friend, older and overweight, far from the all-star baseball pitcher I had known and loved, now the boss of the US Attorney prosecuting the case. He gloated over this high profile victory and shook hands with his VIP cronies who had flown in for a celebration while I, his former best friend, was going to jail, virtually ruined.

I remember what it felt like holding my wife that day. I managed to make a soulful prayer of forgiveness for his spirit, the best friend I had once loved so keenly. I hoped that if this victory gave him completion, that the Lord would release him from his vendetta and provide absolute salvation for his soul. After all, there was another "court" yet to come.

I later learned from the prison counselor that he suspected certain phone calls made to prison officials had been "improper", requesting that my "time" be as hard as they could manufacture. A few good folks told me how wrong they felt it was, including the prison professionals as they carried out orders. It was hard. They made it hard.

In his prison greens, smoking a cigar gifted to him by the late Clement Stone of Success Magazine, President Nixon's former personal assistant blew a smoke circle and intoned, "Berny, you have to remember: in the Bible when Joseph was thrown into that horrible dark well, it was not by strangers, but by his own jealous brothers. Not his best friend. His blood brothers, Berny."

We continued walking a razor-wire fenced track, looking over a prison recreation yard. His Prairie-Home-Companion-like voice had only recently been saying, "This is the President of the United States phoning." Now he said, "Joseph spent years in prison following his slavery. And think of Gandhi, arrested numerous times for such crimes as treason against the state. As a wrongfully accused attorney of the law, he gave patient service against his injustice following his years in prison.

"As dramatic as the incarcerations of Dr. Martin Luther King Jr. and Nelson Mandela were do you believe Dr. King is a crook, Berny? Or Nelson Mandela?"

I shook my head. Of course not.

"If we wonder back as far as Saint Paul we see lots of criminals, and no small number put to death for the framed-up charges brought against them.

"No, B.J.," suggested the President's assistant. "No, you can't understand how Gandhi would free an entire nation of people, how Mandela would change an entire nation's political structure, or how Dr. King would reform the American experience following their own jail time. God has strange and wonderful plans for his people through injustice and long suffering.

"Your job is to keep your faith as you hold on to what is right within our system and our country, and to live by and under the law, leading out front in the hardest job of all, remaining invisible as you lead. Remain invisible standing out front. That is the secret of what comes next for both of us. In our media age, it becomes a learned behavior."

That man, the President's assistant, went on to publish a very successful magazine and then to consult to the largest companies in the world. I still remember the end of the cigar and where it was flipped that day. As the red-hot ember spun through the twilight it felt like a beacon of hope—a flash of flame turned to white, and it dropped out of sight. That is when I realized that my "strange and wonderful plans" had only just begun.

Years later, in the early '90s, my wife, Lynn, and I launched Income Builders International, now known as www.ceospace.biz, to teach entrepreneurs and business professionals crucial lessons of a capitalist society not taught even in the best MBA programs. As a result of my struggles in life we now teach the importance of due diligence and legal compliance in business development, which we provide as a principle of "over-compliance." Combined with principles based on cooperation vs. competition, our Super TeachingTM technologies, which are also being installed in public schools to reform classroom learning and a nationwide radio show dedicated to entrepreneurs, our business owner community has exceeded our expectations as a place where the dreams of entrepreneurs are supported, nurtured, and realized, regardless of their backgrounds.

I can now watch my wife coaching hundreds of CEOs, as our company helps leaders develop billions in funding, win prestigious awards such as the best new automotive product of the year; best new pet product of the year; best new toy product of the year; best new consumer electronic product of the year, to name a few from 2006 and 2007. She remains a shy person and likes best to stay behind all the haza-rah. Still, she is proud when the applause roars for her husband and family. I see it in her expression. You can celebrate redemption for a human life in a look, and I discover it several times over in her eyes.

My sons grew up in a prison greeting room playing UNO with their convict father, and have since spent years around our entrepreneur programs and completed the teen program—Free Enterprise Alternative Systems Training.

They have graduated to defend the laws and freedoms of their nation. When I watched my precious sons greet each other upon Ryan's return from Iraq in 2007 with a Purple Heart, I realized redemption had come from being their father, from learning the lessons of past struggles together

Only now, years later, as CEOs around the world communicate their victories to us, can I make sense of the importance of my journey, especially when we hear of the legal actions that have been avoided due to the over-compliance teachings we have provided. Now, I read dedications to us from famous authors in their books, and receive thanks from successful CEOs, filmmakers and magazine publishers—they even want to make a movie about my story—and I think, redemption comes in one contribution at a time, one leverage at a time, as you never know where God has positioned you to advise and to consent.

Redemption exists in those you inspire to never give up, never slow down, never lose your faith, never cease to wonder at the plan God has for even one sinner's life made whole. The only difference between a life that affects the many versus a life that affects the few resides in the revolution of the soul, in understanding how you see your ability to co-manifest your dreams with God. That is the place of your personal redemption. Perhaps it is just this one single principle that is the secret—faith in your dreams, regardless of the challenges, for if they are inspired they can only come from one place.

Sometimes Lynn and I look over the Elk River in Alabama at the sunset and reflect on the strange and wonderful plans that helped us create companies which span the world. Holding her small hand, I realize that our commitment to our dreams, the inspired ones, and to God is the same. As the sun hits the red soil and shines across the glistening water, I wait to feel Lynn squeeze my hand. Then I know, this is the reason for God's strange and wonderful plans.

HUGH BALLOU

Hugh Ballou is founder of SynerVision International, Inc., an international facilitation, consulting, and training practice in Blacksburg, Virginia. For many years Hugh has been working with leaders in businesses, schools, churches, non-profit organizations, and community groups, leading project teams to find consensus, even with very difficult decisions. Before his full-time work as facilitator, consultant and executive coach, he served as Director of Worship Ministries, staff strategist, and facilitator in churches from 120 to 12,000 members.

In addition to managing project teams as a neutral facilitator, Hugh is also skilled in leading workshops, retreats and seminars on planning, reorganization and goal setting. Hugh has served in leadership roles as a business owner and chamber of commerce president, as a church musician, worship planner and worship leader in various church settings. He has had extensive experience in conflict management, staff relations, multiple staff dynamics, business plans, financial planning and budgeting, complex schedule issues, evaluations of programs and staff performance as well as goal setting.

He has published two books on Transformational Leadership: *Moving Spirits, Building Lives: Church Musician as Transformational Leader* and *Workbook for Transformational Leaders* and numerous articles on Transformational leaders.

Hugh holds a BMu from Georgia State University in Music Literature and an MMu from The University of South Florida in Choral Conducting. He regards facilitation as a skill related to conducting in that the leader mentors, guides, and structures the building of harmonious, unified results while participants use their skills to provide the substance. His studies in facilitation include *Compression Planning* with McNellis Corporation and *Solution Mapping* with Professional Solutions, ToP Facilitation program with the Institute of Cultural Affairs.

Koinonia: A Child
Shall Lead Them

In the summer if 1979, I joined the staff of First Presbyterian Church in
Saint Petersburg, Florida as Director of Music. The church had been
through some transformation that was not the best. In fact, the membership had fallen below 1,000 for the first time in decades. There was not
much spirit or participation in most programs or in worship itself. Some
Sundays, my three children were the only children in childcare during worship. Needless to say, the church was not growing; it was maintaining.

About five years later a dear choir volunteer offered to start a children's
choir during the early worship service, which was held at 8:30 AM. Since some
more children had been showing up occasionally, I agreed. It started with
energy. There was not momentum in this program since there was not much
momentum in the church. A youth leader was hired to develop a youth program. The youth ministry began scheduling Sunday night activities that were
quite amazing. The next year a group of parents came to me and asked why
the children couldn't have the same kind of program. I wondered, "Why
not?" as well.

We held an informational meeting of interested parents and recorded
their ideas. Out of this gathering a new concept was born. We didn't know
what to expect, but it sounded like it would be fun. So we held a series of
summer planning team sessions. The group struggled with the name, and
about approved the name "Kaleidoscope" until the last meeting while review-
ing the logo, which was built around children in a circle holding hands. This
looked like a kaleidoscope, but it also symbolized community. Koinonia, then
was the unanimous choice. We defined our concept as follows:

Koinonia is a children's music and fellowship program seeking to be a religious, educational, artistic and recreational factor in the lives of those who participate in it. Koinonia's purpose is to instill a sense of service, discovery, and fellowship in the participants through carefully planned activities, to encourage a sense of personal responsibility, and to create a sense of community . . . In everything, Koinonia is totally committed to the well-being of its participants and its leaders display faith, guidance, discipline, patience and understanding program-wide. No one can say for sure how deeply the children will be influenced by the program, but to meet the children's basic needs, the program will have to be under the guidance of those whose lives exemplify these qualities

Koinonia come from the Greek and is commonly used to mean "Christian fellowship." In most cases it goes another step and means "building a community of faith." This name turned out to be a blessing to the program and an unspoken guideline for building an unselfish community of sharing, cooperation, and giving not only with the children, but with adults as well. If fact, adults wanted to come just to be present for the energy it gave them.

The goal of the program was "to create an environment that would lead our young people to feel good about coming to church by providing opportunities for fellowship, learning, and service, each of which lead to worship of our Lord and Creator."

From the inception, the idea was to write our own material and choose our own schedule, not to compete with the overall church schedule, but to complement it. The modules each week were somewhat complex in coordinating and in staffing. It ran something like this:

Recreation

Snack Supper

Module I

Module II

Module III

The program was designed to serve children from Kindergarten through grade five. All the children were together for recreation and snack supper, then rotated modules by age group. The modules were **Sing & Rejoice** (choir), **Orff & Stuff** (Orff Schulewerk), and **Discovery** (an explorative module where children discover truths about their faith and their world through storytelling, games, drama, puppets, arts, crafts, and other fun and exciting experiential activities.) The leaders stayed in the same room and the children rotated for each module. The leaders had to develop age appropriate modules for each group. The group agreed from the outset that the program was to remain flexible, adjusting as necessary to insure that the needs of the children were served. We would evaluate it weekly and make the necessary adjustments as needed. It was successful.

The phenomenon that followed was awesome! Every group in the church helped. Members of different committees took a role (Christian Education, Fellowship, Publicity) the governing body, the Session, provided several teachers for the "Discovery" modules, and the Presbyterian Women helped with the snack supper. This was true *koinonia* in its purest sense. But there was still more to come.

As the children shared their gifts in worship, they were not showcased as "cute" and "precious" diversions to the worship. They were full participants in the liturgy and understood their role as leaders in worship. After the first two years, I convinced the pastor to schedule a "Children's Sunday" in the late spring, just before or after Easter. He willingly obliged. To our greatest pleasure, it was a wonderful worship experience. The pastor offered the sermon, but the children led every part of the service, provided the music, and helped usher. As an addition to the day, we hand-colored every bulletin with bright symbols of our faith. These were the symbols we learned about in our discovery together. Every bulletin was an original. Every one was a masterpiece. None were left in the pews after worship to be discarded. They were "keepers."

Week after week, year after year, the program evolved so was never the same, and provided meaningful content and experiences for both the children and the leaders. The momentum of energy the program created was a great opportunity for recruiting and using volunteers.

What made this program work so well? What about it made it easy to find volunteers to fill the leadership roles? What caused the demographics of the church to go from "barely any children in the early 1980s" to "children are the largest demographic in the congregation in the late 1990's"?

I intended from the beginning to share the joy and share the participation. There had to be an overall leader (me), but others "bought in" at a high level of participation. One value was that the program was multi-faceted. It appealed to most kids, even those who didn't think they wanted to sing. They all tried, and most succeeded.

We began with kindergarten and primary age children building transition to adulthood with their joy of coming to church. Koinonia was a good way to reinforce family Christian values and make them automatic. The program grew because it was a quality program with support from students and families. It became known throughout the community as well. We had visitors every week.

Many people were dedicated on many levels: planners, teachers, parent helpers, Session members taught, many helped with publicity—everybody was in it together! It kept its momentum from year to year and did not lose interest over the summer months.

A really important factor was that the leadership rotated from year to year. The leadership team consisted of 10 members each with a specific assignment. Here's a list of team slots:

Chair (one year term after being co-chair one year)

Co-Chair (prep for being chair)

Choir Leader

Choir Leader

Publicity Planner

Snack Supper Coordinator

Orff Leader

Discovery Leader

Christian Education Representative (for coordination)

Parent (to coordinate the Parent Helper Program)

All parts of the body worked together in a true sense of *koinonia*. The children taught us adults what this meant. They didn't draw lines or form sub-groups with special interests. They just had fun! So the adults took note and learned. The program had far-reaching effect, not only in the congregation, but in the community as well. It laid the foundations for the future for its participants. Camaraderie was great—there were no prima donnas—everybody gave 110%. Everybody had the benefit of the program in mind, not their own needs.

So why did this happen this way with no "church wars" or other turf issues? It all sprang from the cooperative spirit of collaboration in the initial planning and in every evaluation thereafter. No change was made without consensus. It sometimes took longer, but the result was long lasting and fulfilling.

The leaders had a passion for doing their best. High achievers inspired others to do their best as well—most of the time without comment—just by setting an example. The idea of developing our own program material was also key. It was more work, but everybody was fully invested in the outcome.

The programs were very successful with little or no dropout over the years. We evaluated it constantly and revised as needed. This truly was a central point of the success. Motivated leaders will invest their time and talent for the success of their project. It was their program, tailored to the particular group we had. That changed from year to year as new faces appeared, but the attendance only rose.

At the end, there were about 100 children in the program and because the church had a good program for children, the largest age demographic for the church was children aged zero to six. That, in itself, was a transition. The largest transition, however, was in the lives of those who participated and in the community of faith itself. God brought us together in a most special way. I did not know about transformational leadership at that time; I didn't know much about *any* type of leadership. I just asked God to bless our efforts as we attempted to follow his will.

The transformation was in the energy that the Koinonia Children's Program brought to the church, and resulted in increased attendance and membership, especially of families with young children.

The real transformation was that the children taught us how to be a community that cared for one another, helped one another and cooperated with one another, no matter what our age, rank, or program affiliation. The children taught us how to celebrate in worship when they stood on the pews and waved their hand-made "Alleluia Wands" (taught to us by a visiting theologian, Glaucia Wilkey) when they heard the words alleluia in the hymns. The taught us how to give when they made sock puppet Christmas gifts for the infirm at home and took them personally and sang Christmas carols and hymns. They taught us how to praise God as they joyfully attended church at any time, but most especially at the time of Koinonia. They were not aware of the transformation. They were unaware of the Greek word or its translation. But they did model true Koinonia for our community of faith.

In true *koinonia*, we were blessed richly.

D. EDWARD STANLEY

D. Edward Stanley was born in Newport News, Virginia in 1955 to Bill and Dee Stanley. Three years later his parents divorced, setting the stage for an extraordinary event.

In 1960, Dee Stanley married Vernon Presley, Elvis Presley's widowed father. David was just four years old, 20 years younger than his new stepbrother when he moved into the Graceland Mansion. Through a strange twist of fate, Elvis Presley had become David's big brother.

Living and growing up at Graceland from 1960 to 1977, David was an integral part of Elvis' daily life as a close family member. He was first exposed to the art of movie making when he was just five years old. Throughout the '60s during his stepbrother's prolific film career, David spent much of his young life growing up on the back lots of film giants like MGM and Paramount. As he watched productions like "Ice Station Zebra" unfold before his eyes, David found himself hooked on the magic of moviemaking.

In the early '70s, David, just 16 years old, dropped out of school to go to work for Elvis as a personal aide and bodyguard. As the youngest bodyguard in the history of Rock and Roll David witnessed the Elvis phenomena first hand. From the King's moments of glory to his tragic demise, David was there, protecting the King from everyone—everyone but the King himself.

Following Elvis' death in '77, David established himself as a successful writer with a New York Times' bestseller, *Elvis We Love You Tender*. His ongoing passion for film guided his decision to study film production during his college years in the 1980s.

Throughout the '90s, David continued to balance his successes as a writer with a drive to direct film. He authored *Raised on Rock* and the *Elvis Encyclopedia,* which continue to sell worldwide. In addition he wrote and produced several documentaries on the rock icon and acted as a technical consultant for a number of movies and television specials.

David marked his directorial debut in 2006 with "Protecting the King" and is currently initiating pre-production activities on his second feature film "Restoring My Father's Honor". D. Edward lives in Dallas, Texas and is president of Impello Films, Inc.

PROTECTING THE KING

Interview with D. Edward Stanley

Hugh: **David, can you describe the situation in which the transformation occurred?**

David: I started Impello Films five years ago. I put together a plan of action, followed it, and we've had success since we've done that. We didn't have a major change, we just set out with a solid plan of action, strategically laid out, surrounded ourselves with good people, delegated the expertise to those who are experts in their fields, and the next thing we knew, we had a major feature film, "Protecting the King," which will be released this year in the United States.

Hugh: **That's a major transformation!**

David: To me transformation means that you've gone from one thing to another and created something different. For us I guess, if you want to call it a transformation, you can call it a mindset. We had an overall plan of action and created an end result. A successful end result.

Hugh: **You have a vision! The transformation is bringing the vision to reality.**

David: OK, I guess we can term it a transformation from that perspective. I would call it follow-through, persistence and moving one step forward. I came up with the idea for the film "Protecting the King" back in the 1980s. I had already written the script, and finally when I sat down and decided to create Impello Films, which would be the company that would own the intellectual property, that's when we began to put together our plan of action. We understood that we had to put together a solid business plan communicating our objectives within the structure of putting the film in the market place—How're we going to do it? What is the intellectual property? Who would own the intellectual property?—something that our investors could look at, comprehend, and understand as far as what they get when they do invest. Taking it from there, which means raising the money then going into what we call preproduction, which was casting, pulling together the production crew—about 120 people on staff, for about three months to make this picture a reality. After we shot the film, we went into "post," which involves pulling together your sound guys, your music guys, your editors, your color separators . . . . That's all the things we had structured when we began our adventure of the project of making "Protecting the King" with Impello Films.

I can see that the transformation was that we went from page to stage, mind to marketplace. We had an idea, we took that idea and pushed it forward through, I think, good planning, strong organization, implementation, and incredible passion, which turned it into a reality.

Hugh: **Speak more about the passion element.**

David: Well, passion is the key to anything. I feel a lot of people that are in the work force who don't have a passion for what they are doing are missing the key. I am fortunate enough to have a product that's driven by passion. I try to tell every individual that I come into contact with that that passion is inside your heart—that one thing that you really want to do—or that series of things, which means sequence, start with that one thing and then build on that. With our project, we had had a story that we thought was a great film and the passion to make it and the passion to reach the level of the major film market was what drove us over the top and made it a reality. A lot of people just get up and go to work in a mundane way—and that's good. "A man is worthy of his hire." And the necessity of doing it is something that people are driven by. I try to be with people who seek that inner passion that is inside their heart and the more they let that flow out, the more they let that passion drive them. That defines their purpose and then they have a clear-cut vision of where they want to go and what they want to do. I think that gives them the courage to step out of their box and make their dream come true.

Prior to filmmaking, I did a lot of success-conditioning coaching, what I share with you is what I share with them. Take that passion, driven by purpose, driven by a focused vision, seeing it clearly in your mind, and turn it into a reality. I think that's a true transformation.

Hugh: **Comments on the list of traits of a Transformational Leader, realizing that all of them may not apply.**

David: Delegate, that's the bottom line. Within the structure of my company in the film business, obviously the Director, Producer, Writer, which are the roles I play, are things that I have a passion for, and these are things that I was qualified to do. But even though I had the knowledge to do it, it was very important to put a team around me that could make that vision a reality. That is, I am a director, this was my directorial debut within the structure of a major motion picture. I have done stuff for BBC, The History Channel and various other documentaries, but this was my first feature. So as a quote "director," the most important thing to me was to surround myself and delegate responsibilities to my director of photography, which was the guy who was to make sure that all the camera angles were set. We storyboarded everything to create that situation prior to going on the set and shooting. My first and second assistant directors who make sure that everything's in place—all actors, all lighting, all sound guys, all extras—any and everything that has to do with a single shot is done by that first and second assistant director. Delegating to them make my responsibilities a lot easier. Within the structure of producing, Scott Vandiver and Gail Lynn were producers on the film. Gail's a highly motivated organizational professional I'm not. I'm a creative, directive type. I'm a producer overseeing everything that's going on, but delegated those responsibilities to Scott, who had experience within the structure of film production, and then you had Gail, who was an overall organizational professional. So delegation is an absolute key. Don't try to do everything. Don't think you own everything. Don't think you know everything. The most important thing about any property or product or endeavor that anyone can enter, is open up with a teachable spirit and delegate to those who are experts in the structure of their field.

Hugh: **How do you encourage others to take initiative, to contribute ideas, to take risks.**

David: Well, in my case, everything that happened with Impello Films in its first venture within the structure of "Protecting the King," was driven by passion. My investors invested and believed in David Stanley because of my overwhelming passion for the project and my leadership quality of taking team players and making it a reality. The team of players that worked with me, the cast and crew, the people that did post production and sound, the extras, all the way down to the caterer. They were driven and highly motivated by the passion that the director, in this case, me, had for the project. They see passion. They see vision. Those things are catching. And those things are absolutely crucial and essential to any success. There has to be a leader who is driven by passion and purpose. They saw my passion. They saw me take risks. They saw me as the leader who was the captain of the ship. Leadership is everything. And you go back to delegation. Sometimes you have to delegate leadership. A lot of people have great concepts and ideas but they are not driven by a passion and a purpose. They need to find somebody who is. Sometimes that means stepping back and checking your ego at the front door and allowing the others, who *are* driven by the passion and the purpose to drive the overall project.

Hugh: **Talk about your relationship with others who work with you in terms of coaching for success and reinforcing the things that are good.**

David: Basically a pat on the back is worth 10,000 miles. It's like I saw in the movie "Patton." They said if you give George Patton a headline, he's good for another 500 yards. It all about encouragement, it's all about quality control. It's also about that person who's driving the ship having the clear-cut vision of knowing just what he or she wants or doesn't want. Communicating that objective to the individuals that are working with you and around you is absolutely crucial. If an individual is on the team who doesn't get it, then the individual doesn't need to be on the team. Those individuals have to have a teachable spirit as much as the individual who is leading has a teachable spirit. Both come together creating a win/win scenario for everybody. So leadership and communicating your objectives to individuals so they can see your passion and purpose and understanding that you know, as the leader, as the passion guy, as the quest holder, that you are the individual that has the vision and conveying that vision to them. Communication is key. You have to be able to communicate with everyone who works with your company. Whether you are delegating, even when they are delegating from the delegation, you have to have your thumb on top everything. I'm not talking about micromanagement. I'm talking about a clear-cut vision of exactly what you want. What you expect.

Hugh: **In tough times, when you didn't get what you expected, how did you interact with team members encourage them, to coach them and to build them up?**

David: I don't know if you want this answer. First, I'd go up to them and sit down and say, "What's the deal? Let's work this thing out." Second, if they didn't do it the second time, I'd say, "This is not an issue, this has to be done. We've got a situation." Third, if the situation is out of hand, they have to be replaced. That's basically the way I handled it. There were a half dozen people that came and went because they just didn't get it. And that happens in the workforce anywhere. Anytime you are in a situation as a leader, you encounter people that just want a paycheck, and there's nothing wrong with that. If it's one of the situations where responsibility is an absolute crucial element to success of that company or project, you can't tolerate anything less than the best they have. If they don't have that, then their passion is not in it, their passion is somewhere else. I encourage them to go find that passion and succeed in that other field or adventure and/or venture that they are passionate about.

Hugh **How does that speak to the overall energy for the overall project?**

David: It lifts the spirits of everyone else because that are all driven by the passion and they feel great about what they are doing and they see someone that's pulling it down. It's one thing to have a lack of knowledge and not quite comprehend what's going on. It's another thing to have all the knowledge and not be driven by the passion and the purpose.

That's why your team needs a clear-cut vision. Everybody has to see the same results. We're all in it as a team together turning it into a reality.

When I was working on this project as producer/director, there were some tough times. "I need you to do it this way. I really need you to do it this way. If you don't do it this way, get off my set!" It really got down to that in a couple of situations. Even after that happened, that individual came bad to thank me for knowing what I wanted. "You know what you want. You're not persuaded by those who think they know what you should or shouldn't do. You have a vision." OK, Hugh, it's the vision. It's the vision that you have that's impenetrable, it is set, it is locked, and you are on course and nothing gets in the way. And when it does, you use diplomacy. You hold hands. You talk business. You do your best. When it doesn't work out, then you say goodbye.

When I'm spending $250,000 a day, it's going to be right. There is no question. There is no lack of involvement. It's either, "you're in it or you're not." You're either with it or you're not. Those are the kinds of teams that drive a highly successful project.

Hugh: **You speak of your personal faith and the gifts and opportunities God has given you. How do those empower you as a visionary, transformational leader?**

David: My faith is real important to me. I am one of those who is always very candid. I am not ashamed of the gospel. I never have been. Since my transformation from the old David to the new one—I was 12 years old—I have been driven by my faith. I always know that "Greater is he that is in me than is in the world." No matter what situation that may arise, my faith and the Creator of my faith drives me and comforts me knowing that all things can be done by those who give honor to God. I believe that we are born with a talent, we are born with a gift, and it's important to use that gift. I don't know if he will take it away, but I see a lot of people who are fired up and have a clear-cut vision. Give it to them. I think the world is full of sin, but the biggest sin is to have a God-given gift and not use it. I believe this. I have done a lot of successful things in my life as a media marketing consultant, I've been a success-conditioning coach, then I took the big step to shut down those businesses to break into film. This was a tremendous step. Thousands do it every day. Thousands crash and burn every day. I had that vision driven by purpose and placed in my heart through my faith in God, and it's turned into a reality.

Hugh: **What advice would you have for leaders who are undertaking a project to transform an organization or transforming a vision into a reality?**

David: I think the most important thing to do when a project begins is to check your qualifications. Number one: Are you a leader? This is the bottom line. A leader is a person who is driven by a vision, a passion, and a purpose. They have the ability to convey their message to a team of people who get it—who catch the vision—who grab the passion. They have the ability to do that. They have the ability to take their concept or idea and put it into the mainstream marketplace through that communication. They have to be the kind of person who can stand in a room and people look at you and say, "I want to follow this guy's lead because I see and feel his passion and I am driven by his purpose and I want to be a part of that success." So the number one thing to do before starting something like this is to check your capabilities. Go through the checklist of your own skills. And don't forget to check your ego at the door.

For example, Gail Lynn has worked for me for five years. She is an organizational expert. She's a leader in her field. She's not a producer/director. She does produce and lead. She doesn't do what I do. She feels the vision of what I do and takes it to heart. She takes that vision and conveys it to the people who work for her. She has a leadership quality. If you don't have a leadership quality, then team up with someone who does and let them convey the message. Those who are in the trenches, so to say, their decision never blurs. It's always the same. Whatever it takes to get there with integrity and humility, just push forward. And you learn and delegate and find out any and every thing you can to make it a reality. What I didn't know about film, I learned. What I couldn't comprehend, I read. What I couldn't read, I studied. Become an expert in what you want to do. Let the passion drive you. And let the purpose solidify your heart and you'll get there a lot quicker.

Hugh: **How would you summarize all this?**

David: If you dream it, you can do it. Of course, B.J. Dohrmann teaches us to believe in dreams coming true. The summary is very simple, you get the passion, the vision, in other words, you get what you want to do. You have heard me speak and say "What do you want to do when you grow up?" Let me solidify what that is. When you do that, do what's necessary with integrity and humility to make it a reality. And that's resources, that's sequence, that's communication, that's learning. It all goes back to where I started this conversation. Success is driven by a teachable spirit. Have a teachable spirit. What you don't know, you can learn. What you can learn you can duplicate. What you can duplicate, you can turn into reality. The reality can make that vision and that dream come true. There's no real big secret to it. The bottom line is you have not because you ask not. You have to get up and do. Any success is driven by doers—people who get up and do something every day to get closer to the goal of success in their life— no matter what that goal is.

VERNON SANDERS

Vernon Sanders has been a rock musician, a college professor, a jazz pianist, a non-profit arts foundation administrator, an author, and a music publisher. He served for many years as Associate Professor/Director of Choral Activities at the University of Regina, Canada, and most recently was Director of Music Ministry at Trinity Presbyterian Church in San Carlos, California for 16 years before "retiring" to devote more time to his family and his position as publisher of Creator Magazine. His education includes degrees in Music Education and Musicology from UCLA, and a DMA in Conducting from Stanford University. He was the founding president of the Saskatchewan Choral Federation, and the founding Charter Member of the Association of Canadian Choral Conductors. His published choral works appear in a number of catalogs, and choirs under his direction have appeared on regional and national radio and television in the United States and Canada. He is a frequent clinician throughout North America. He has served on the staff and the board of the Schuyler Institute for Arts in Worship and the National Association of Church Musicians. Dr. Sanders is known for building program, encouraging people, and cultivating the skills of volunteers within a context that promotes sensitivity to their primary role as worship leaders. He "unretired" in October, 2005, to answer a "missionary" call to develop the worship ministry of a small church that had identified lack of a meaningful worship as an inhibitor to their vision of fulfilling the Great Commission. He currently serves as Director of Worship at First Presbyterian Church in Grover Beach, California.

THE CHURCH MUSICIAN AS TRANSFORMATIONAL LEADER: CAN THIS CHURCH BE SAVED?

There is an ongoing feature in the *Ladies Home Journal* that asks "Can this Marriage be Saved?" In it, both parties outline the problems in the relationship as they see them, and then a therapist evaluates the relationship and answers the big question.

While we at *Creator* are not in any doubt that "the church" can be saved, we know that many individual churches face critical decisions, the resolution of which often leads to the survival or failure of that particular congregation. We took the opportunity to ask a number of church musicians how, and whether the musical leadership and/or decisions were able to transform churches at which they had served, or were serving. The answers, from a geographical, denominational, and "worship style" cross section of North American churches were instructive. The experiences have been woven into a composite first person narrative for convenience. Several specific responses have been highlighted in sidebars.

The Arrival

"They Want Me To Fix It"

Here's my story: When I arrived at the church my first day, I already had some history with them. I knew the pastor, and had met one of the ruling elders

149

during the negotiation process. The board had had a consultant in because they felt that their church was "stalled" at an attendance plateau, and they were vaguely unhappy with their worship. The consultant, with whom I was acquainted, had worked with a small group from the congregation, as well as some of the staff, to explore the scriptural basis for worship. The consultant also did a "worship education" weekend that culminated in a first for the congregation—a unified worship service designed around pre-determined "behavioral objectives" linked to the morning's scripture.

When the consultant finished, the board and pastor had a "laundry list" job description for a new position—Director of Worship. They wanted the existing worship staff to stay in place if at all possible, but they were looking for somebody to come in and fill a "super producer" role—essentially to create a top layer appointment to vision and guide the church's worship life. The consultant put me in touch with the church, and we began a dialogue that led to a call.

In other words, they wanted me to fix it. Of course, how you define "it" became the issue in the days to come.

"This Is Hard Work"

I got here in the fall, after the new season started, but well enough before Christmas so that I could select the "big piece," which was a classical work with professional brass. First rehearsal, first problem: "This is in Latin." *Yes it is.* "We've never done Latin before. I don't like Latin." *That's ok . . . you'll do fine.*

The choir and band were in rough shape. Musical discipline was an issue. Even more important, the prevailing corporate culture was to question everything—choice of music, the need for more than one hour a week in rehearsal, you name it. The carpet was red, the choir robes were green, and there was a television ministry. Fortunately it was cable access, because anyone who watched it must have been colorblind or just blind.

The robes came off; first, once in a while when the service was more casual, then because we were doing an anthem where the anthem was sung unexpectedly from within the congregation, then all together for the summer. At the end of the summer, they only went back on for "festival" services, and the video crew thought I knew what I was doing.

As the choir worked on the Christmas cantata, they began to see that matching vowels, and unifying consonants made a difference in the communication of the message. The congregation began to compliment them on how good they sounded. The choir began to feel good about their efforts, and began to work harder to get better. Now they were being asked to do music of different styles (the previous director was "stuck" in a particular anthem vocabulary), and to differentiate between a classic choir sound and a "radio" sound for the more contemporary pieces. The band accompanied the choir regularly, though not often, and they needed to adjust to that ("The drums are too loud." *Fine . . . let's have you move to the other end of the row. Better now?*)

At the cantata presentation, the addition of the brass raised the singers to the next level, and astounded the congregation, which had never had professional players appear in worship. They discovered that one can make a living as a trumpet player and still be a Christian. They also discovered that they were moved beyond belief, even though the piece was in Latin. We "explained" the text to the congregation by having them speak it in unison before the choir presented a movement, and then singing one or more hymns with the same or similar text after the movement. We never told the congregation what we were singing about. But they got it.

After the service, the choirmember who had been the biggest (and continuing) opponent of Latin confronted me. "That was hard work." *I know.* "But it was worth it. I learned to love that piece." *Thank you.*

The Process

"Now I Understand"

For the first year, I had no advocate except the pastor. The youth director had a lay elder, as did the children's director. But circumstances didn't permit one for worship. The previous elder for worship was convinced that no one could do the job better than himself, and by the end of his term, didn't speak to any of the music staff. When I arrived, a "caretaker" elder was in place, but he left after a few months, overwhelmed by the enormity of the task as he understood it. The next elder became unexpectedly transferred out of town within weeks of accepting the position and he had to resign. Months went by with no help. Still the worship staff team pressed on.

As part of my interview process, I asked the existing staff what their roles were, and how they thought they were doing. The answers were predictably cautious, and self-serving. Then I asked them to tell me, if they could design their own job description, with no restrictions, and do only what they were passionate about, what would that look like?

Suddenly faces lit up, and the body language changed. One wanted to write music for the congregation. One wanted to do children's music, and felt stuck in the adult music department. One wanted to go to school, and work less hours. One wanted to learn to design worship services. Everybody wanted to learn.

I asked them all to write up their "perfect" job description, and promised that I would do everything possible to let them do what they desired. Amazingly, they all chose to re-assign themselves—some slightly, some significantly—to other jobs. They had become "burnt out" in their current tasks, and wanted new challenges. Even more impressive was the fact that they were all qualified (in some cases overqualified) for the roles they were suggesting for themselves. Most impressive of all was that no one wanted to do the job that I wanted to do and was hired to do—vision and empower them as leaders.

At the same time, I changed the language when talking to the choir from "performance" to "worship leadership." We regularly reinforced their role as worship leaders, and the modeling that they needed to do for and on behalf of the congregation as a result of their new, more scriptural role. The choir began to see that their "part" of the service didn't begin and end with the anthem, but included leading congregational hymn singing, parking as far away as possible from the front door of the sanctuary so that all the spaces weren't filled an hour before everyone else arrived, and reaching out to new visitors that they recognized from their position on the platform.

Finally, the nominating committee found a potential worship elder. I was mortified that they hadn't asked me for suggestions, and astounded at the person who was being recommended. I asked for a meeting, in order to satisfy myself that God was at work in this process.

What was scheduled as a one hour "meet and greet" turned out to be a five hour, in depth exploration of the scriptural reasons for worship, the role of the elder, and a rather intense discussion of why it cost so much money. As the conversation went on, I could sense that this person's heart was in the right place, but that he had no "heart" for worship. He felt called to be an elder, but, he confessed, he would rather serve another portfolio, because, in response to the same questions I asked to the worship staff, that was where his passion lay. As it turned out, the elder currently holding that portfolio would, I felt, be a great worship elder. Some further discussions, a lot of prayer, and some measure of surprise later, he assumed the other portfolio, and I got the worship elder I would have chosen from the beginning.

In the process of this discernment, the candidate and I pondered some tough questions, including trust of paid staff. When the dust had settled, but before he accepted the non-worship portfolio, he said "Now I understand. I came in here wanting to reign you in. I leave here supporting these goals entirely."

The Players

"I've got your back"

Along the way, the rest of the elder board was pressed into voting (twice) to re-affirm the process. Each time the vote was unanimous. Each time we took the time to revisit the goals and tried to re-intrepret those goals to those who were either unclear, unappreciative, or unsupportive. I believe that this re-interpretive process will be continual, for change frightens some people, and makes most people uncomfortable.

What we learned is that trying to "tweak" things (Can we use less drums? Should we change the time of the service? Do we need to stop using the projection system?) doesn't end the whining, but it takes a lot of effort away from our stated core value of providing excellence in worship as a tool for outreach to the de-churched. As our carryover congregation has aged, some of them feel threatened by the influx of new, younger members, and are concerned about themselves being ignored or left out.

Even though each service intentionally selects the most appropriate music from a very wide variety of styles, we've learned that, in the immortal words of Ricky Nelson, "you can't please everyone, so you have to please yourself."

Without the support of the pastor, the transition would have ground to a stop at any one of many points. As part of the hiring process, we agreed that any disagreement that we might have would be kept strictly behind closed doors. When we leave his or my office, we are united. I have his back, he has mine. The congregation, though some have tried, can't use "divide and conquer" tactics.

The youth director has been on board from the beginning, as she sees the expansion of musical styles as inclusive for the population she serves—those under the age of 20. We now do periodic "Rock the Pews" worship/concerts on weekday evenings, where the band gets to "turn it up." Paired with events that naturally draw families with young children, we are seeing attendance that rivals a Sunday morning worship service, and worship participation which has been heretofore unknown for this congregation.

The Transformation

"I like it." " Thank you."

Slowly but surely, the perceived direction of the congregation has slowed from its previous course toward an aging demographic that was shrinking for no other reason than simple mortality tables. Each week now we see visitors, many with young children. Because this is primarily a "retirement" community, most people who move here are either searching for a new church home or de-churched, and exploring whether joining a congregation will assist the transition to their new community.

Worship services are now more intergenerational, vibrant, and alive—the energy spills out into the fellowship time. There is a growing sense of congregational mission. During advent, for instance, the board decided to purchase some door hangers to promote the congregation's seasonal events. Two Sundays were set aside to distribute the door hangers to those in the congregation who would be willing to place them according to a specific set of instructions: *One at each house on either side of you, and the three houses directly across the street from you.*

With a "manageable" task, the door hangers were snapped up before the first day was over. During the week that followed, many people came in asking for more, even though they were gone, including a real estate broker in the congregation who volunteered to place them on every door in a new development. More meaningfully, people also came in with stories of how the door hangers allowed them to meet their neighbors, and issue personal invitations.

The following Sunday we were overwhelmed . . . to the point where there was literally no place to park for blocks around and people were observed driving away. In response, the elder for evangelism arranged for valet parking attendants to be on site for the next week. People are now visiting mid-week during the day, asking about worship, and the church, because they've "heard this is a great church."

What changed? People's attitudes.

Why did their attitudes change? I believe it is because they now recognize the excellence in worship, and they have something to invite people to that is "special."

To a certain extent, modern culture requires differentiation in order to be noticed. If things are "ordinary" the common perception is that they are unworthy of being explored—"nothing is happening here." I do not advocate spectacle for spectacle's sake—but rather that the intentionality of excellence, inclusion, variety, spontaneity, and subtext brought to music and worship can provide an atmosphere where people can begin to encounter the living God.

For too long, we as worship leaders—pastors and musicians—have worried about "pleasing" people. Too many debates and too many terminations of employment can be traced to disagreement about "what" should be in the service. The resolution of the "what" debate is probably far into the future.

At the same time, few are asking the "why" question. Too often the "what" is determined by "it worked at XX so it should work here," or "they are doing it down the street, so all we have to do is that and it will work for us too." The "why" question is the hardest to answer. I have observed that the churches who ask "why" before "what" are generally more successful, and, ironically become "what" models.

I personally believe that the "how" conversations are sorely lacking as well. Too often those on either side of the "what" debate don't engage in or listen to any "how" dialogue. When there is genuine effort to understand "why" then "how" easily determines "what."

Simply put, not everyone can be Willow Creek, or Saddleback, or First Baptist, Brooklyn Tab, or Peachtree. On the other hand, every single church in North America has the ability and the capability to transform themselves into something that reaches people—either more people, or more deeply, or more widely across generational, racial, or ethnic boundaries, or more often, or more intentionally, or more . . . .

I believe in what *Creator* has been saying: Local solutions for local situations. It worked for us.

In our case, the journey and the task are far from over. Transformation is a process, not a conclusion. For as we transform those who are here, we also transform those who are newly arrived, and transform our community as well. For us, the signs are evident—in the tears running down the faces of those touched by a worship service centered around the presentation of a classical Mass, in the spontaneous rising of the congregation as the band cranks into another gear at a key change, in the renewed commitment to serving at the local soup kitchen, in the willingness to dream of more ministry by relying on faith in passing budgets with small deficits, in the ease in which strangers say to the pastors at the local coffee shop, "I know you! You're on TV. I like it." "Thank you."

And that's my story.

fine

BISHOP KOBEE FITZGERALD

Bishop Kobee Fitzgerald was born February 11, 1974 in Town Creek, Alabama to Elijah and Annie Fitzgerald, the youngest of six siblings. He was united in Holy Matrimony to Katenia Dozier on June 12, 1993, and to their union they have been blessed with three adorable daughters. He holds an Associates Degree in Pre-Secondary Education, Bachelor of Arts in Religion/Philosophy, and currently a Senior at the Interdenominational Theological Center in Atlanta, Georgia pursuing a Masters of Divinity Degree. He committed to the call of ministry in May 1993 and began leading a local congregation in September 1994. As he grew in wisdom and in the things of God, he began to hear the voice of God clearer, calling him from the traditions of men. In January 2000, Bishop stepped out of the box with Pastor Katenia and God's Word as lamp unto his feet. Together they prayerfully founded Ekklesia Missionary Baptist Church (Ekklesia means **"called out"**). In April 2002, God spoke clearly to identify as "Ekklesia—A Spirit-filled, Christ Centered, New Creation Church." Feeling a conviction for apostolic order in need of mentoring, relationship, and impartation, Bishop Fitzgerald became a covenant pastor/spiritual son with Apostle Maurice K. and Lady Brenda Wright. Since that time, Apostle Wright has confirmed and given direction, releasing the man of God to fulfill his purpose on the earth. He was consecrated to the office of Bishop on November 10, 2002.

EKKLESIA MINISTRIES

E
kklesia Ministries was founded January 1, 2000 with five charter members. My vision for an empowering and transforming ministry was birthed out of years of frustration with mundane religious activities that left people void of hope and daring to dream. With this eagerness and refusal to accept business as usual, I began writing the preferred future (vision). It had to be crafted in such a way that it would invoke change, eradicate complacency, while holding true to the great commission.

Matthew 28:19-20 says, "Go to the people of all nations and make them my disciples. Baptize them in the name of the Father, the Son, and the Holy Spirit, and teach them to do everything I have told you. I will be with you always, even until the end of the world." (CEV) With help from my mentors I compiled the following vision statement:

> We exist to make the Kingdom of God visible upon the earth, maintaining a Christ Centered, Spirit Filled, New Creation Church, making disciples through balanced biblical preaching and teaching, working with a spirit of excellence through effective team ministry, building people of purpose, power, and praise which possess wholeness for living and eternal life.

Any leader knows that change is often combated with fear and old paradigms, which are not easily replaced. Therefore, I recognized that continued education was a must for both myself, and the laity. I began seeking others who could mentor us and openly share both their success and failures. I also found other ministries to shadow and serve as models for our vision. I found this help at United Christian Church in Gadsden, Alabama, where the senior pastor is Maurice K. Wright, and at the Daystar Tabernacle International in Douglasville, Georgia, where the senior pastor is Halton Skip Horton.

After two years of rehearsing our purpose, the people began to invest in the mission with their time, talents, and resources like never before. However, this only provided provision, but did not fulfill the stated vision. True enough, it sounded like and looked like the vision inside the four walls, but that wasn't enough. So we began to think of ways to empower people to truly possess wholeness. Since most of the people attending had experienced the new birth and laid claim to eternal life, external wholeness was needed. Spiritual wholeness and centeredness is paramount, but living beneath our God-given potential yet makes one impoverished.

Therefore, in January 2002 we opened the Ekklesia Child Development Center with before- and after-school care. This gave us the ability to offer free, subsidized, and low cost childcare while encouraging persons to empower themselves through education. At the same time we provided a needed service to our community. This aided the empowerment process tremendously and created a morale that soon spread throughout our spiritual family and beyond. Laid off plant workers went back to school and became certified in Childcare Management. Members donated furnishings and worked to transform the space into an appreciated center. God also sent special people along who always knew exactly what we needed to know. One of such persons was Deborah Humphrey. Her tireless work will never be forgotten. To this day, the center continues to grow and flourish under our excellent leadership team. Leaders like Katenia Fitzgerald and Shirley Sullivan are truly God-sent.

With such excitement in the air we began looking for new possibilities; knowing the sky was the limit. In May 2003 we opened Manna Restaurant, which was managed by an all-volunteer staff providing breakfast, lunch, and dinner to our community. Due to its tremendous success and popularity we decided to use it as employment opportunities and financial empowerment. Manna is currently being relocated into our own building, which will house everything under one roof and be more cost efficient, leaving resources for new projects.

One of the most exciting things about all that is happening here is the group of people making the vision a reality. We are truly blessed to have 20% of our congregation who are a part of the "baby boomers" generation. The other 80% are "Generation X." Maybe we should call them "Generation NeXt." These statistics tell us we have the first generation of "unchurched" youth. Something special is happening here. We recognize that, and know that there is still hope for the future. I'm sure the question is, "Why are they coming and sharing in your vision?" I am convinced that it is because we have learned to listen and to follow Jesus' model for reaching people. In the words of Howard Thurman in his work *Jesus and The Disinhierted*, Jesus always reached out to those outside the margins. Many times youth and young adults are pushed to margins and considered invaluable or bracketed as tomorrow's leaders. Yet I have learned that everyone has something great to contribute in the family of God. We have developed a model of inclusive ministry, which detests classism, sexism, racism, and ageism. Adults and youth work hand-in-hand to accomplish our mandate, including vision planning, and implementation. If you provide a place, they will come; and if you give them a voice they will stay and bring a greater vitality.

Transformation is happening one life at a time. I'm not sure what the future holds for Ekklesia, but I know it involves changes. As the world changes around us so do the needs of individuals. Therefore we have developed a culture that now embraces change to accomplish our vision. Empowering others to lead and to learn has made a significant impact in the Shoals Area.

DANIEL T. BENEDICT, JR.

D aniel Benedict served for twelve years as the Director of Worship Resources at the General Board of Discipleship and is now retired and living in Hawaii where he continues to write, consult, teach online, and travel to lecture. His books include *Come to the Waters*, *Contemporary Worship for the 21st Century*, and, the most recent, *Patterned by Grace: How the Liturgy Shapes Us*.

CHANGING LANES: TRANFORMATIONAL LEADERS LISTENING TO THE SPIRIT IN CONTEXT

I n spite of the emotional attachment to the "way things are," the church is always challenged to change. When churches refuse to change, they die, whether it is doctrine, practices, or who it considers to be its neighbors. Whether speaking of the universal church or the local church, change comes because the risen Christ goes ahead of us into Galilee, "and there you will see him." (Mark 16:7) "Galilee" was and is the place of Jesus' ministry—the context where the living One encounters people and God's new creation, the reign of God that we pray for, comes into being.

Chula Vista, California, just south of San Diego, was "Galilee" for the people of Chula Vista First United Methodist Church. The congregation formed and located itself in the new town's center in the early 1900s. As Chula Vista grew and its perimeter expanded in the 1950s, the congregation changed lanes and moved to what was then the edge of town at Third and J Streets, building larger facilities to accommodate the new population of the city. By the mid 1980s Chula Vista was again growing dramatically, now to the east because San Diego Bay was its western border. The annual conference had designated the East Lake development a priority for the location of a new church, but funds for this were not available.

That in brief was the outward context, but what inward dynamic would connect this to following Christ into this "Galilee"?

On January 1, 1986, I was appointed pastor of the church. I came with experience and a vision of discipleship known to the early Methodists in their class meetings where in love they were accountable to each other for keeping the General Rules—doing no harm, doing good, and using the means of grace. (See the 2004 *Book of Discipline,* ¶ 103, pp. 72-73.) The heart of that 18th-century practice of holiness was now called Covenant Discipleship. Dr. David Watson, staff on the General Board of Discipleship of The United Methodist Church, provided vision and resources for introducing and supporting this approach to serious accountability for shared discipleship. In 1984 and 1985 at Covina United Methodist Church, my previous appointment, the congregation had experienced a dramatic response to the invitation to "watch over each other in love," as Wesley had described the central dynamic of the class meeting. Over eighty people (more than ten percent of the congregation) responded to the invitation to be accountable for their discipleship, and they met weekly in twenty-two groups. I came to Chula Vista hoping for a similar response.

Shortly after arriving, I proposed starting a "pilot group" to test drive the model. Thankfully, there was enough responded that two groups were formed. In six months the participants were convinced of the soundness and effectiveness of Covenant Discipleship (CD) groups and were ready and willing to serve as temporary leaders of new groups. We invited David Watson to come to Chula Vista for a "CD weekend." He gave biblical and historical reflection on Jesus' call to discipleship on Friday and Saturday, and on Sunday he preached and invited any and all, if they felt called by Christ, to come to the chancel rail and declare their intent to be accountable disciples. Sixty plus responded and met immediately after the morning worship services to self-select a group that met at a time suited to their schedule. Pilot group members served as temporary leaders until each group had written its specific covenant based on the General Rules and had become familiar with the dynamics of the group meetings.

Every group's covenant was unique, but there was two standard clauses for all group covenants: "I will heed the warnings of the Holy Spirit not to sin against God and neighbor," and "I will obey the promptings of the Holy Spirit to serve God and neighbor." It was common for group members to wonder, "What in the world is a 'prompting of the Spirit'? How would I recognize a prompting? How do I know it is not just my imagination or my own self-projections?" In time and with group reflection, members gained ability to discern "warnings" and "promptings" and to trust their sense of the Spirit's leading.

These promptings were sometimes more than strictly personal. Sometimes these covenant disciples had promptings that involved the congregation and its mission. Specifically, some began to ask questions about what it meant for the church that fifty thousand new homes were scheduled for construction in East Lake and other large developments expanding the city eastward. They were "listening" as they saw new thoroughfares, fire stations, malls and a Home Depot being built. They wondered if the Spirit was prompting CVFUMC to help a new congregation to get started in the midst of all those new homes, or if the church should consider relocating from its present increasingly "invisible" site to a location visible to the traffic in and out of these new neighborhoods.

Then a rather dramatic offer came. A large supermarket chain, which had an old and inadequate store across the street from the present Third and J church site, approached the church leaders and offered to buy a portion of unused land on its current seven acre site. The pastor and leaders agree to consider it. After a few months, the supermarket chain returned with a proposal to buy the whole property for a little over three million dollars. Suddenly, those who were discerning the prompting about response to East Lake were faced with questions: Is this God's provision for relocating the church? Is this a temptation? How would we sell the existing property, buy land, build new facilities, and continue to have a place to meet in the interim?

By now, these were not private ruminations. Some of the pioneers in discipleship were also elected leaders in the congregation and now were bold to ask church members to live their baptismal covenant to "accept the freedom and power God gives you" and to "put your whole trust in [Jesus Christ]" promising to "serve him in union with *the church which Christ has opened to people of all ages, nations and races*." (See "The Baptismal Covenant I" in *The United Methodist Hymnal*, p. 34.) They brought their promptings about the church's mission to the Administrative Board, where the response of some was swift and angry. To some, changing lanes was not acceptable. To others, it seemed very risky. Many wondered why "this congregation" should shoulder the burden of new neighbors—let the Annual Conference plant a church "out there." Many expressed feelings of being robbed of the familiar by a company ready to pay big bucks for "our church."

Now "warnings" took on new significance, as people took sides on the issue of sale of the property. Even CD group members found themselves divided on the matter of relocation and felt pulled into the vortex of demonizing those with whom they disagreed. "I will heed the warnings of the Spirit not to sin against God and neighbor" became a lived struggle.

In a few months, leaders pushed through the fear and moved forward to meet with the District Building and Location Committee, the city's building department, and potential lenders. Resistance to the whole matter continued, but increasingly the will to move forward with our being in mission in a growing community persisted. Feasibility questions that dogged the prompting were answered. A five and a half acre site located on a major artery into and out of East Lake was available. The supermarket offer was shaped to include agreement to advance 1.5 million dollars to buy the new site and allow the congregation to continue to use the present location until the new facilities were built. It also included provision for the church to take from the existing buildings anything that it wanted to include in the new church building.

Here another prompting was obeyed: take the stained glass, pews and furnishings, and the pipe organ in order to maximize the current congregation's sense of continuity, especially those who were grieving the loss of their familiar church home.

Key lay leaders lived out their covenant in carrying the project forward. Preliminary drawings were prepared. The buyer's agreement was firmed up. The district's building and location committee's criterion were met. Loans were lined up. Literature that interpreted and explained the relocation was distributed to all members. Now it was time to decide.

A date was set for a "church conference" so that all members would have opportunity to vote on the question: shall Chula Vista First United Methodist relocate to the proposed site? The worship space was full on this Sunday afternoon. Members who had not been in church for years came out to vote. With deliberate care the plan in its detail was again laid out, questions were asked, and then the vote was taken. The decision to relocate passed by two votes. Could a divided house stand? Was this too close a vote to proceed? All were stunned by the close outcome. When Bishop Jack Tuell called me the next day to find out how the vote went, he paused after hearing of the closeness of the vote and then said, "Well Dan, that will take a lot of pastoral care." He was, of course, frighteningly correct.

But the pastoral care did not fall to the pastoral staff alone. Members cared for one another. Here again, the promptings of the Holy Spirit to serve God and neighbor were obeyed. Still, some members left the church, but most stayed and began to live through grief, finding acceptance and living into what it meant to change lanes heading toward "Galilee." Frequently, the promptings were to have faith and to trust that if God was asking this of us, then we needed to be alert to look and listen to where God was providing the way forward.

Leaders now turned their efforts to finalizing plans, conducting the "Expanding Horizons" campaign with the assistance of a professional fund raising company, producing an interpretive video, and planning a congregational dinner where members would make a pledge toward a two million dollar capital campaign. One woman felt prompted to pay for the cost of the congregational dinner to be held at a harbor-side restaurant so that no one would have to pay for coming to a meal where they were going to be asked to make a financial commitment to the new church project.

Anticipating the vision's reality, a service of hope and dedication was held on the bare land. In February 1993, I was appointed to serve as staff with the General Board of Discipleship, but the leaders God had raised up—listening, visionary, courageous leaders—were in place to see the *transactional process* to completion so that the congregation could engage in a *transformational ministry* of reaching out to people in an expanded community.

The relocation was completed in late 1995 with a dedication in the winter of 1996. Today the church is reaching out and growing, touching the lives of people in both English and Spanish language ministries. Covenant Discipleship groups continue to meet in accountability for the core disciplines of Christian living. By taking seriously these basic disciplines, they serve as transformational leaders, whether or not they are appointed or elected to some office. They simply pay attention in their context and change lanes at the prompting of the Spirit. Such change feels extraordinary at the time, but in the long view, it is just the way the reign of God comes among us.